ABOLITION & RECONSTRUCTION

ABOLITION & RECONSTRUCTION
AN EMERGENT GUIDE FOR COLLECTIVE STUDY

The W.E.B. Du Bois Movement School for Abolition & Reconstruction

Philadelphia, PA
Brooklyn, NY
commonnotions.org

Abolition and Reconstruction: An Emergent Guide for Collective Study
The W.E.B. Du Bois Movement School for Abolition and Reconstruction

Texts reprinted with publisher permissions. We thank Seven Stories, Verso, *Spectre Journal*, *Truthout*, and Hood Communist for their invaluable work in publishing essential abolitionist writings.

ISBN: 978-1-945335-36-5
eBook ISBN: 978-1-945335-37-2
10 9 8 7 6 5 4 3 2 1

Common Notions
c/o Interference Archive
314 7th St.
Brooklyn, NY 11215

Common Notions
c/o Making Worlds Bookstore
210 S. 45th St.
Philadelphia, PA 19104

www.commonnotions.org
info@commonnotions.org

Discounted bulk quantities of our books are available for organizing, educational, or fundraising purposes. Please contact Common Notions at the address above for more information.

Cover design by Josh MacPhee
Layout design and typesetting by Suba Murugan

CONTENTS

INTRODUCTION

The W.E.B. Du Bois Movement School for Abolition & Reconstruction

MAKING THE ROAD AS WE WALK IT

What you are holding in your hands is not a finished product. But it *is* the product of the first year of our work at the Du Bois Movement School. And what a year it has been. The Du Bois Movement School was the product of a particular time and place. We came together amid the long wake of the 2020 rebellions, which mobilized hundreds of thousands nationwide and pushed abolitionist narratives into the mainstream. This raised pressing questions for abolitionists across the country and the world, and more than any other, the question was this: what do we *mean* when we say abolition?

The system had two responses to this question: co-optation and counterinsurgency. While sectors of the political and media apparatus have embraced the language of abolition (and decolonization) to water down and co-opt them, the state has also subjected revolutionary abolitionists to severe repression—we experienced both in Philly. In this context, we engaged in conversations among movement educators and radical organizers across the city to ask what kind of political education would help to take abolitionist struggles to the next level. We realized that this required not only training in concrete organizing skills but real understanding of the world, history, economics, and power. We realized that we need to study our world if we want to change it.

Our team of five facilitators came to this task from very different backgrounds and bringing different skills—from youth organizing, historical preservation, formal and informal education spaces, to revolutionary theory and organizing, and cultural memory work. Our weekly seminars brought together more than 120 aspiring organizers across two semesters for intensive study, participatory conversations, and community building. But as soon as we began, the terrain shifted again, dramatically. The Palestinian liberation movement exploded on October 7th, reorienting and reinvigorating mass struggle across the country and beyond. And then, one of our own comrade-facilitators, Ant Smith, was sentenced and sent to federal prison—another target of the long post-2020 counterinsurgency.

So while we were sticking and moving, we were also rolling with the punches, teaching by learning and learning by teaching, experimenting and improvising, "making the road as we walk it" as Mexico's Zapatistas describe it. Improvisation isn't chaos, however, it's exploring variations on a theme, and we should be clear that this guide—and our political orientation—builds on some clear themes. While we offer a non-sectarian overview of the historical emergence of capitalism, colonialism, white supremacy, patriarchy, policing, and prisons, we often speak in terms of four fundamental principles that guide our work:

- We are *abolitionists*: we don't seek to reform carceral structures, we seek to destroy them. But we also know that there can be no true abolition without a profound process of reconstruction—no tearing down of carceral structures without building up alternatives.

- We are *internationalists*: the structures we confront—colonialism, slavery, white supremacy, patriarchy, and capitalism—are fundamentally global, and so too must abolition and reconstruction be grounded in the transnational solidarities and the revolutionary struggles of the present.
- Our analysis is *intersectional*: our carceral world operates through the complex interplay of race, class, gender, and other categories. But against the liberal co-optation of intersectionality, rather than any simple intersection, we see this concept as describing the complex historical intertwining and contemporary entanglements of these oppressive structures.
- We engage in *participatory* education: we study the world not simply to understand it, but to change it by strengthening the leadership of oppressed communities. Participatory political education doesn't simply fill students with preexisting knowledge—it's a collective project to change ourselves as we change the world.

These four elements are inseparable from one another. For example, abolition as reconstruction means building the kind of egalitarian and non-carceral world that is *only* possible when we think globally, when we take different parameters of domination seriously, and when we understand that the people themselves are the foundation of all change. Toward that end, we don't simply *study* intersectionality and internationalism: we put them into practice by creating a non-hierarchical and healing space that brings together aspiring organizers from many different communities across the city.

If this process begins from our own individual experiences, it doesn't end there. Instead, the experiences we bring from different communities and different experiences of oppression provide the raw materials for study, but like any materials they need to be *worked*. In our seminars, we do that work collectively, sharing experiences, drawing connections between them, and mapping out the systemic relations underpinning them. In the process, we expand our understanding of oppression and domination, we grasp its different parameters and manifestations, and above all we do so *together* in ways that build *knowlegde* and *solidarity* at the same time. The systems we confront don't want us to study, and they definitely don't want us to study together.

How to Use this Guide

This guide provides a framework for 12 weeks of study on revolutionary abolition, decolonization, and struggle past and present. It contains several elements that can be used in different ways:

- Short weekly readings
- Study questions to guide conversation
- A facilitator guide with basic takeaways from the readings and suggestions for participatory activities

In practice, we supplemented these with additional suggested readings and content, powerpoint slides with study questions and additional background, and the rich knowledge, examples, and clarifications offered by our facilitation team. While our 2-hour sessions often took different forms, with modules shifting around up to the last minute, they often held to a basic structure that looked something like this.

Sample Session (2 hours)	
15 minutes	Introductions and grounding: • How are we feeling in one word? • What's motivating and inspiring us today?
15 minutes	Collective recap of last week's conversation: • Take a moment to look at your notes, dig into the readings, and begin to think. • This is a process of reinforcement.
20 minutes	First participatory activity, can be: • Breakout conversations • Collective mapping • Gallery walk
10 minutes	Collective reportback
15 minutes	Break for food and connection
30 minutes	Political education module, can be: • Turn briefly to your neighbors • Breakout groups to answer study questions • Large group collective conversation • Facilitators filling in basic takeaways
15 minutes	Transitioning out, looking forward, announcements

What We Have Learned So Far

We have learned more in the past year than we could hope to document here, in part because it is difficult to express what it means to hold and feel a space collectively, to take the temperature on the fly and shift direction, to know when to ask questions and when to provide answers, when to lead and when to follow, how to value contributions while pushing back. But here are some key approaches, techniques, and methods we have developed:

- *Build people up early.* Everyone is capable of study and intellectual work, but reading and studying is hard, and we should welcome that. Let participants know that they won't get everything the first time, and that's completely normal–it's why we work together and return to the material repeatedly. Emphasize that it's OK to not understand, to be wrong, and to ask questions. The earlier participants begin to speak, the more likely they are to continue.
- *Develop community agreements and norms.* In our first sessions, we collectively discuss and decide what kind of space we want to create and how we want to relate to each other. Often this involves guidelines like: step up, step back; WAIT (why am I talking?); take others at their best, not their worst; stories stay, lessons leave.
- *Balance voices.* This can be tricky, and while establishing community norms helps, we found it necessary to establish specific practices for some breakout groups: take a minute to gather your thoughts and write notes, then everyone makes a contribution before open discussion.
- *Hold space for study.* It's always tempting to see immediate organizing tasks as the most urgent thing, and we definitely felt this when mobilizations against the unfolding genocide in Gaza were a daily phenomenon. But remember that we hold space for study for a reason–to think about and analyze what's happening at the moment, but also to build for what's beyond that immediate moment.
- *Build on local context and history.* Philadelphia is central to our curriculum and conversations, and we are always looking for ways to make our own location a central reference point for our work. Be on the lookout for local histories, community memory,

and ongoing struggles that can be incorporated into study and action.

- *Take advantage of facilitator strengths.* Every member of our team brought unique skills, knowledges, and experiences to our seminar. Try to take advantage of those strengths while balancing specialization with a coherent curriculum and ensuring that every facilitator can deliver the baseline. This can look like particular examples in conversation to illustrate a concept, or a short presentation on a specific area of interest or expertise.
- *Timekeeping is easy, interrupting rich conversations is hard.* We struggled with timekeeping, and it always seemed like we were running out of time. This is because every conversation, every experience and perspective shared collectively brought an incredible richness to our seminar that we were hesitant to cut off. But try to be disciplined with keeping to the schedule, and above all *start on time.*
- *Group project.* For our second cohort, we incorporated a group project on the legacies of colonialism. Groups chose a country from a hat and met outside seminar to prepare a presentation on the impacts of colonialism, resistance against it, and to gather texts, film, and music associated with the struggle. The project deepened connections and created friendships that we know will last.
- *Audiovisual enrichment.* Always be on the lookout for film clips, art, music, and spoken word. Provoke thought by asking for reactions to a militant painting, song, or film.
- *Collecting chants, practicing affirmations.* Conclude your final week of study by reinforcing and affirming the connections that have been built, upholding those who have contributed, and collectively rehearsing chants contributed by participants themselves.

This guide is not an end but a beginning. Please connect with us to let us know how it works for you, what works and what doesn't. We will be revising this guide for future editions and incorporating insights from our incoming cohorts, so your feedback is crucial. In the meantime, please use these texts, questions, and facilitation guide to let a thousand seminars and study groups bloom.

Abolition Means Revolution

As revolutionaries, we are permanently caught between upsurge and downturn, explosive resistance and repression. It is in these in-between moments that political education and organizing are most essential: sharpening our analytic weapons and building our movements in preparation for the next moment of possibility. At the Du Bois Movement School, we do both, seeing collective study *as* organizing in the face of global imperialism, creeping fascism, and ongoing genocide.

This means pushing back against those who seek to water down abolition and make it compatible with the status quo, and also against those who dismiss abolitionist organizing as inherently reformist. Why? Because abolition means an unrelenting attack on the oppressive structures that function most directly to uphold capitalist white supremacist patriarchy, and because we know as students of history what's possible when those institutions are attacked and weakened. This means insisting that abolition is about far more than police and prisons: it's about abolishing global capitalism, imperialism, patriarchy, and white supremacy. Abolition means border abolition, the abolition of the military-industrial complex, and decolonization here and abroad. Abolition means building solidarity worldwide, it means community power and self-defense, and it means building a world of social, racial, and gender equality.

In other words, we insist that abolition is revolutionary in part by doing what we can to make it revolutionary in practice. And if we know anything at all, it is that this process begins and will be led by poor and oppressed communities themselves and the struggles they unleash.

What's the call? Free 'em all!

Philadelphia,
August 2024

1 | WHO ARE WE? WHAT IS KNOWLEDGE?

Study Questions:

1. How do our experiences become knowledge?
2. Who are you? Why are you here?
3. What does Gramsci mean when he says we are all intellectuals?
4. What does a revolutionary abolitionist intellectual *do*?

Key Concepts:

- Traditional Intellectual: professors, religious leaders, media figures, political leaders, and others who work to justify and legitimize the existing status quo.
- Organic Intellectual: those intellectuals who provide new arguments to reshape common sense in either reactionary capitalist-neoliberal or revolutionary-abolitionist directions.
- Hegemony: a form of power exercised through civil society, ideas, and common sense, rather than the direct, violent coercion of the state (but which helps to uphold the state).
- Counter-hegemony: the development *and institutionalization* of new ideas that point toward a different society, through political parties and new forms of intellectual production and education.

Antonio Gramsci, *The Prison Notebooks* (1929–1935)

Are intellectuals an autonomous and independent social group, or does every social group have its own particular specialized category of intellectuals? The problem is a complex one, because of the variety of forms assumed to date by the real historical process of formation of the different categories of intellectuals. The most important of these forms are two:

1. Every social group, coming into existence on the original terrain of an essential function in the world of economic production, creates together with itself, *organically*, one or more strata of intellectuals which give it homogeneity and an awareness of its own function not only in the economic but also in the social and political fields. The capitalist entrepreneur creates alongside himself the industrial technician, the specialist in political economy, the organizers of a new culture, of a new legal system, etc. . . .
2. However, every "essential" social group which emerges into history out of the preceding economic structure, and as an expression of a development of this structure, has found (at least in all of history up to the present) categories of intellectuals already in existence and which seemed indeed to represent an historical continuity uninterrupted even by the most complicated and radical changes in political and social forms. The most typical of these categories of intellectuals is that of the ecclesiastics, who for a long time . . . held a monopoly of a number of important services: religious ideology, that is the philosophy and science of the age, together with schools, education, morality, justice, charity, good works, etc . . . these *traditional* intellectuals. . . .

All men are intellectuals, one could therefore say: but not all men have in society the function of intellectuals. . . .[1]

When one distinguishes between intellectuals and non-intellectuals, one is referring in reality only to the immediate social function of the professional category of the intellectuals, that is, one has in mind the direction in which their specific professional activity is weighted, whether towards intellectual elaboration or towards muscular-nervous effort. This means that, although one can speak of intellectuals, one cannot speak of non-intellectuals, because non-intellectuals do not exist. But even the relationship between efforts of intellectual-cerebral elaboration and muscular-nervous effort is not always the same, so that there are varying degrees of specific intellectual activity. There is no human activity from which every form of intellectual participation can be excluded: *homo faber* cannot be separated from *homo sapiens*. Each man, finally, outside his professional activity, carries on some form of intellectual activity, that is, he is a "philosopher," an artist, a man of taste, he participates in a particular conception of the world, has a conscious line of moral conduct, and therefore contributes to sustain a conception of the world or to modify it, that is, to bring into being new modes of thought.

The problem of creating a new stratum of intellectuals consists therefore in the critical elaboration of the intellectual activity that exists in everyone at a certain degree of development. . . . What we can do, for the moment, is to fix two major superstructural "levels": the one that can be called "civil society," that is the ensemble of organisms commonly called "private," and that of "political society" or "the State." These two levels correspond on the one hand to

1. Thus, because it can happen that everyone at some time fries a couple of eggs or sews up a tear in a jacket, we do not necessarily say that everyone is a cook or a tailor.

the function of "hegemony" which the dominant group exercises throughout society and on the other hand to that of "direct domination" or command exercised through the State and "juridical" government. The functions in question are precisely organizational and connective. The intellectuals are the dominant group's "deputies" exercising the subaltern functions of social hegemony and political government. These comprise:

1. The "spontaneous" consent given by the great masses of the population to the general direction imposed on social life by the dominant fundamental group; this consent is "historically" caused by the prestige (and consequent confidence) which the dominant group enjoys because of its position and function in the world of production.
2. The apparatus of state coercive power which "legally" enforces discipline on those groups who do not "consent" either actively or passively. This apparatus is, however, constituted for the whole of society in anticipation of moments of crisis of command and direction when spontaneous consent has failed.

Karl Marx, "Introduction to A Contribution to the Critique" (1844)

The weapon of criticism cannot, of course, replace criticism by weapons, material force must be overthrown by material force; but theory also becomes a material force as soon as it has gripped the masses. Theory is capable of gripping the masses as soon as it demonstrates *ad hominem*, and it demonstrates *ad hominem* as soon as it becomes radical. To be radical is to grasp the root of the matter. But for man the root is man himself.

Toni Cade Bambara, *Deep Sightings & Rescue Missions* (1996)

I became acquainted with folks who demonstrated that their real work was creating value in the neighborhoods—bookstores, communal gardens, think tanks, arts-and-crafts programs, community organizer training, photography workshops. Many of them had what I call second sight—the ability to make reasoned calls to the community to create protective spaces wherein people could theorize and practice toward future sovereignty, while at the same time watching out for the sharks, the next wave of repression, or the next smear campaign, and preparing for it.

Insubordinates, dissidents, iconoclasts, oppositionists, change agents, radicals, and revolutionaries. They studied, they argued, they investigated. They had fire, they had analyses, they had standards. They had respect for children, the elders, and traditions of struggle. They imparted language for rendering the confusing intelligible, for naming the things that warped us, and for clarifying the complex and often contradictory nature of resistance . . . the real work was creating value in the neighborhoods . . . equipping [us] to practice freedom in preparation for collective self-governance. . . .

2 | WHAT ARE WE UP AGAINST?

Study Questions:

1. What oppressive systems do we confront every day?
2. How do they relate to one another?
3. What is a materialist analysis?

Key Concepts:

- Materialism: an approach to understanding the world that emphasizes *not* ideas (idealism), but the concrete things we do in the world, the way we live, and the things we create.
- Mode of Production: the overarching structure of this arrangement in a given place or time (key examples: "primitive" communism, slavery, feudalism, capitalism).
- Means of Production: the ingredients of production, including people but also tools, factories, raw materials, land, computers, etc.
- Forces of Production: the ability of human societies to produce things we want or need at any given moment in history (i.e. technological level)
- Relations of Production: the rules governing how we relate to the means of production, crucially who owns them and how production happens.

- Capitalism: a system of *wage labor* characterized by the extraction of *surplus value*: everything produced by the worker that they don't receive as part of their wage (thus becoming *profit*).

Karl Marx, "Theses on Feuerbach" (1845)

Thesis 1. The chief defect of all hitherto existing materialism—that of Feuerbach included—is that the thing, reality, sensuousness, is conceived only in the form of *the object or of contemplation*, but not as *sensuous human activity, practice*, not subjectively. Hence, in contradistinction to materialism, the active side was developed abstractly by idealism—which, of course, does not know real, sensuous activity as such. Feuerbach wants sensuous objects, really distinct from the thought objects, but he does not conceive human activity itself as objective activity. . . . Hence he does not grasp the significance of "revolutionary," of "practical-critical," activity.

Thesis 2. The question whether objective truth can be attributed to human thinking is not a question of theory but is a practical question. Man must prove the truth—i.e. the reality and power, the this-sidedness of his thinking in practice. The dispute over the reality or non-reality of thinking that is isolated from practice is a purely *scholastic* question.

Thesis 3. The materialist doctrine concerning the changing of circumstances and upbringing forgets that circumstances are changed by men and that it is essential to educate the educator himself. This doctrine must, therefore, divide society into two parts, one of which is superior to society. The coincidence of the changing of circumstances and of human activity or self-changing can be conceived and rationally understood only as *revolutionary practice*. . . .

<u>Thesis 6</u>. But the human essence is no abstraction inherent in each single individual. In its reality it is the ensemble of the social relations. . . .

<u>Thesis 8</u>. All social life is essentially practical. All mysteries which lead theory to mysticism find their rational solution in human practice and in the comprehension of this practice.

<u>Thesis 9</u>. The highest point reached by contemplative materialism, that is, materialism which does not comprehend sensuousness as practical activity, is contemplation of single individuals and of civil society.

<u>Thesis 10</u>. The standpoint of the old materialism is civil society; the standpoint of the new is human society, or social humanity.

<u>Thesis 11</u>. The philosophers have only interpreted the world . . . *the point is to change it.*

Paulo Freire, *Pedagogy of the Oppressed* (1970)

The central problem is this: How can the oppressed, as divided, unauthentic beings, participate in developing the pedagogy of their liberation? Only as they discover themselves to be "hosts" of the oppressor can they contribute to the midwifery of their liberating pedagogy. As long as they live in the duality in which *to be* is *to be like,* and *to be like* is *to be like the oppressor,* this contribution is impossible. The pedagogy of the oppressed is an instrument for their critical discovery that both they and their oppressors are manifestations of dehumanization.

[. . .]

A Note from the Du Bois Movement School: representatives of the Paulo Freire estate do not allow any quotation or extract use from *The Pedagogy of the Oppressed,* and so we were unable to reprint the passages we study, which we consider deeply ironic and an insult to Freire's teaching and legacy. The entire text is scanned and available on various websites. Please read your favorite passages of *Pedagogy* with special attention to pages 48–49, 50–51, 54–55.

Here is the essence of what he argues. We exist in a material reality much like what Marx lays out, and so "education" can't simply be understood as seeking to change ideas. Freire refuses both an "objectivism" which sees us as incapable of transforming the world and a "subjectivism" which sees changing ideas as enough, in favor of what he describes as "subjectivity and objectivity in constant dialectical relationship." What does that look like in practice? Especially in a situation where we don't control the official educational structure, it means understanding the difference between "systematic education"—which requires political power—and "educational projects," which are the starting point of organizing the oppressed *themselves* to build and claim that power.

3 | THE HISTORY OF CLASS STRUGGLE

Study Questions:

- What moves history, and how?
- How do Marx and Engels understand historical progress?
- Why do they describe the bourgeoisie, and capitalism itself, as "revolutionary"?
- What is the difference between "primitive" communism and "modern" communism?

Key Concepts:

- Dialectics: the dynamic movement of history through opposition, conflict, and struggle.
- Bourgeoisie: the owners of the means of production and employers of wage labor.
- Proletariat: those with no access to the means of production, who must therefore sell their labor to survive.
- Surplus Value: what workers produce but aren't paid for = extracted labor = profit.

Marx & Engels, *The Communist Manifesto* (1848)

Chapter 1: Bourgeoisie and Proletarians.[1]

The history of all hitherto existing society[2] is the history of class struggles.

Freeman and slave, patrician and plebeian, lord and serf, guild-master and journeyman, in a word, oppressor and oppressed, stood in constant opposition to one another, carried on an uninterrupted, now hidden, now open fight, a fight that each time ended, either in a revolutionary reconstitution of society at large, or in the common ruin of the contending classes. . . .

The modern bourgeois society that has sprouted from the ruins of feudal society has not done away with class antagonisms. It has but established new classes, new conditions of oppression, new forms of struggle in place of the old ones.

Our epoch, the epoch of the bourgeoisie, possesses, however, this distinct feature: it has simplified class antagonisms. Society as a whole is more and more splitting up into two great hostile camps,

---

1. By bourgeoisie is meant the class of modern capitalists, owners of the means of social production and employers of wage labor. By proletariat, the class of modern wage laborers who, having no means of production of their own, are reduced to selling their labor power in order to live [Engels, 1888 edition].
2. That is, all *written* history. In 1847, the pre-history of society, the social organization existing previous to recorded history, was all but unknown. Since then, August von Haxthausen (1792–1866) discovered common ownership of land in Russia, Georg Ludwig von Maurer proved it to be the social foundation from which all Teutonic races started in history, and, by and by, village communities were found to be, or to have been, the primitive form of society everywhere from India to Ireland. The inner organization of this primitive communistic society was laid bare, in its typical form, by Lewis Henry Morgan's (1818–1881) crowning discovery of the true nature of the gens and its relation to the tribe. With the dissolution of the primeval communities, society begins to be differentiated into separate and finally antagonistic classes [Engels, 1888 edition].

into two great classes directly facing each other—Bourgeoisie and Proletariat.

From the serfs of the Middle Ages sprang the chartered burghers of the earliest towns. From these burgesses the first elements of the bourgeoisie were developed.

The discovery of America, the rounding of the Cape, opened up fresh ground for the rising bourgeoisie. The East-Indian and Chinese markets, the colonization of America, trade with the colonies, the increase in the means of exchange and in commodities generally, gave to commerce, to navigation, to industry, an impulse never before known, and thereby, to the revolutionary element in the tottering feudal society, a rapid development.

The feudal system of industry, in which industrial production was monopolized by closed guilds, now no longer sufficed for the growing wants of the new markets. The manufacturing system took its place. . . . Meantime the markets kept ever growing, the demand ever rising. Even manufacturer no longer sufficed. Thereupon, steam and machinery revolutionized industrial production. The place of manufacture was taken by the giant, Modern Industry; the place of the industrial middle class by industrial millionaires, the leaders of the whole industrial armies, the modern bourgeois. . . .

Modern industry has established the world market, for which the discovery of America paved the way. This market has given an immense development to commerce, to navigation, to communication by land. This development has, in its turn, reacted on the extension of industry; and in proportion as industry, commerce, navigation, railways extended, in the same proportion the bourgeoisie developed, increased its capital, and pushed into the background every class handed down from the Middle Ages.

We see, therefore, how the modern bourgeoisie is itself the product of a long course of development, of a series of revolutions in the modes of production and of exchange. Each step in the development of the bourgeoisie was accompanied by a corresponding political advance of that class . . . the bourgeoisie has at last, since the establishment of Modern Industry and of the world market, conquered for itself, in the modern representative State, exclusive political sway. The executive of the modern state is but a committee for managing the common affairs of the whole bourgeoisie.

The bourgeoisie, historically, has played a most revolutionary part. . . . The bourgeoisie, wherever it has got the upper hand, has put an end to all feudal, patriarchal, idyllic relations. It has pitilessly torn asunder the motley feudal ties that bound man to his "natural superiors," and has left remaining no other nexus between man and man than naked self-interest, than callous "cash payment". It has drowned the most heavenly ecstasies of religious fervor, of chivalrous enthusiasm, of philistine sentimentalism, in the icy water of egotistical calculation. It has resolved personal worth into exchange value, and in place of the numberless indefeasible chartered freedoms, has set up that single, unconscionable freedom — Free Trade. In one word, for exploitation, veiled by religious and political illusions, it has substituted naked, shameless, direct, brutal exploitation.

The bourgeoisie has stripped of its halo every occupation hitherto honored and looked up to with reverent awe. It has converted the physician, the lawyer, the priest, the poet, the man of science, into its paid wage laborers. The bourgeoisie has torn away from the family its sentimental veil, and has reduced the family relation to a mere money relation. . . .

The bourgeoisie cannot exist without constantly revolutionizing the instruments of production, and thereby the relations of production, and with them the whole relations of society. Conservation of the old modes of production in unaltered form, was, on the contrary, the first condition of existence for all earlier industrial classes. Constant revolutionizing of production, uninterrupted disturbance of all social conditions, everlasting uncertainty and agitation distinguish the bourgeois epoch from all earlier ones. All fixed, fast-frozen relations, with their train of ancient and venerable prejudices and opinions, are swept away, all new-formed ones become antiquated before they can ossify. All that is solid melts into air, all that is holy is profaned, and man is at last compelled to face with sober senses his real conditions of life, and his relations with his kind.

The need of a constantly expanding market for its products chases the bourgeoisie over the entire surface of the globe. It must nestle everywhere, settle everywhere, establish connections everywhere. . . . The bourgeoisie, by the rapid improvement of all instruments of production, by the immensely facilitated means of communication, draws all, even the most barbarian, nations into civilization. . . . In one word, it creates a world after its own image. . . . The bourgeoisie, during its rule of scarce one hundred years, has created more massive and more colossal productive forces than have all preceding generations together. . . .

We see then: the means of production and of exchange, on whose foundation the bourgeoisie built itself up, were generated in feudal society. At a certain stage in the development of these means of production and of exchange, the conditions under which feudal society produced and exchanged, the feudal organization of agriculture and manufacturing industry, in one word, the feudal relations of property became no longer compatible with the already developed productive forces; they became so many fetters. They had to be burst asunder; they were burst asunder.

Into their place stepped free competition, accompanied by a social and political constitution adapted in it, and the economic and political sway of the bourgeois class.

A similar movement is going on before our own eyes. Modern bourgeois society, with its relations of production, of exchange and of property, a society that has conjured up such gigantic means of production and of exchange, is like the sorcerer who is no longer able to control the powers of the nether world whom he has called up by his spells. . . . The weapons with which the bourgeoisie felled feudalism to the ground are now turned against the bourgeoisie itself.

But not only has the bourgeoisie forged the weapons that bring death to itself; it has also called into existence the men who are to wield those weapons—the modern working class—the proletarians. In proportion as the bourgeoisie, i.e., capital, is developed, in the same proportion is the proletariat, the modern working class, developed—a class of laborers, who live only so long as they find work, and who find work only so long as their labor increases capital. These laborers, who must sell themselves piecemeal, are a commodity. . . .

All previous historical movements were movements of minorities, or in the interest of minorities. The proletarian movement is the self-conscious, independent movement of the immense majority, in the interest of the immense majority. The proletariat, the lowest stratum of our present society, cannot stir, cannot raise itself up, without the whole superincumbent strata of official society being sprung into the air. . . .

The Black Panther Party for Self-Defense, Ten Point Program (1966)

1. **We want freedom. We want power to determine the destiny of our black and oppressed communities.** We believe that black and oppressed people will not be free until we are able to determine

our destinies in our own communities ourselves, by fully controlling all the institutions which exist in our communities.

2. **We want full employment for our people.** We believe that the federal government is responsible and obligated to give every person employment or a guaranteed income. We believe that if the American businessmen will not give full employment, then the technology and means of production should be taken from the businessmen and placed in the community so that the people of the community can organize and employ all of its people and give a high standard of living.
3. **We want an end to the robbery by the capitalist of our black and oppressed communities.** We believe that this racist government has robbed us and now we are demanding the overdue debt of forty acres and two mules. Forty acres and two mules were promised 100 years ago as restitution for slave labor and mass murder of black people. We will accept the payment in currency which will be distributed to our many communities. The American racist has taken part in the slaughter of over fifty million black people. Therefore, we feel this is a modest demand that we make.
4. **We want decent housing, fit for the shelter of human beings.** We believe that if the landlords will not give decent housing to our Black and oppressed communities, then the housing and the land should be made into cooperatives so that the people in our communities, with government aid, can build and make decent housing for the people.
5. **We want education for our people that exposes the true nature of this decadent American society. We want education that teaches us our true history and our role in the present-day society.** We believe in an educational system that will give to our people a knowledge of self. If you do not have knowledge of yourself and

your position in the society and the world, then you will have little chance to know anything else.

6. **We want completely free health care for all black and oppressed people.** We believe that the government must provide, free of charge, for the people, health facilities which will not only treat our illnesses, most of which have come about as a result of our oppression, but which will also develop preventative medical programs to guarantee our future survival. We believe that mass health education and research programs must be developed to give all black and oppressed people access to advanced scientific and medical information, so we may provide ourselves with proper medical attention and care.
7. **We want an immediate end to police brutality and murder of black people, other people of color, all oppressed people inside the United States.** We believe that the racist and fascist government of the United States uses its domestic enforcement agencies to carry out its program of oppression against black people, other people of color and poor people inside the United States. We believe it is our right, therefore, to defend ourselves against such armed forces, and that all black and oppressed people should be armed for self-defense of our homes and communities against these fascist police forces.
8. **We want an immediate end to all wars of aggression.** We believe that the various conflicts which exist around the world stem directly from the aggressive desires of the U.S. ruling circle and government to force its domination upon the oppressed people of the world. We believe that if the U.S. government or its lackeys do not cease these aggressive wars that it is the right of the people to defend themselves by any means necessary against their aggressors.

9. **We want freedom for all black and poor oppressed people now held in U.S. federal, state, county, city and military prisons and jails. We want trials by a jury of peers for all persons charged with so-called crimes under the laws of this country.** We believe that the many black and poor oppressed people now held in U.S. prisons and jails have not received fair and impartial trials under a racist and fascist judicial system and should be free from incarceration. We believe in the ultimate elimination of all wretched, inhuman penal institutions, because the masses of men and women imprisoned inside the United States or by the U.S. military are the victims of oppressive conditions which are the real cause of their imprisonment. We believe that when persons are brought to trial that they must be guaranteed, by the United States, juries of their peers, attorneys of their choice and freedom from imprisonment while awaiting trials.
10. **We want land, bread, housing, education, clothing, justice, peace and people's community control of modern technology.** When in the course of human events, it becomes necessary for one people to dissolve the political bands which have connected them with another, and to assume, among the powers of the earth, the separate and equal station to which the laws of nature and nature's God entitle them, a decent respect to the opinions of mankind requires that they should declare the causes which impel them to the separation.

We hold these truths to be self-evident, that all men are created equal; that they are endowed by their Creator with certain unalienable rights; that among these are life, liberty, and the pursuit of happiness. That, to secure these rights, governments are instituted among men, deriving their just powers from the consent of the governed; that, whenever any form of government becomes destructive of these ends, it is the right of the people to alter or to abolish it, and to institute a new government, laying its foundation on such principles, and organizing its powers in such form, as to them shall seem most likely to effect their safety and happiness. Prudence, indeed, will dictate that governments long established should not be changed for light and transient causes; and, accordingly, all experience hath shown that mankind are more disposed to suffer, while evils are sufferable, than to right themselves by abolishing the forms to which they are accustomed. But, when a long train of abuses and usurpations, pursuing invariably the same object, evinces a design to reduce them under absolute despotism, it is their right, it is their duty, to throw off such government, and to provide new guards for their future security.

The Combahee River Collective Statement (1977)

Part 2. What We Believe

Above all else, our politics initially sprang from the shared belief that Black women are inherently valuable, that our liberation is a necessity not as an adjunct to somebody else's may because of our need as human persons for autonomy. This may seem so obvious as to sound simplistic, but it is apparent that no other ostensibly progressive movement has ever considered our specific oppression as a priority or worked seriously for the ending of that oppression. Merely naming the pejorative stereotypes attributed to Black women (e.g. mammy, matriarch, Sapphire, whore, bulldagger), let alone cataloguing the cruel, often murderous, treatment we receive, indicates how little value has been placed upon our lives during four centuries of bondage in the Western hemisphere. We realize that the only people who care enough about us to work consistently for our liberation are us. Our politics evolve from a healthy love for ourselves, our sisters and our community which allows us to continue our struggle and work.

This focusing upon our own oppression is embodied in the concept of identity politics. We believe that the most profound and potentially most radical politics come directly out of our own identity, as opposed to working to end somebody else's oppression. In the case of Black women this is a particularly repugnant, dangerous, threatening, and therefore revolutionary concept because it is obvious from looking at all the political movements that have preceded us that anyone is more worthy of liberation than ourselves. We reject pedestals, queenhood, and walking ten paces behind. To be recognized as human, levelly human, is enough.

We believe that sexual politics under patriarchy is as pervasive in Black women's lives as are the politics of class and race. We also often find it difficult to separate race from class from sex oppression because in our lives they are most often experienced simultaneously. We know that there is such a thing as racial-sexual oppression which is neither solely racial nor solely sexual, e.g., the history of rape of Black women by white men as a weapon of political repression.

Although we are feminists and Lesbians, we feel solidarity with progressive Black men and do not advocate the fractionalization that white women who are separatists demand. Our situation as Black people necessitates that we have solidarity around the fact of race, which white women of course do not need to have with white men, unless it is their negative solidarity as racial oppressors. We struggle together with Black men against racism, while we also struggle with Black men about sexism.

We realize that the liberation of all oppressed peoples necessitates the destruction of the political-economic systems of capitalism and imperialism as well as patriarchy. We are socialists because we believe that work must be organized for the collective benefit of those who do the work and create the products, and not for the profit of the bosses. Material resources must be equally distributed among those who create these resources. We are not convinced, however, that a socialist revolution that is not also a feminist and anti-racist revolution will guarantee our liberation. We have arrived at the necessity for developing an understanding of class relationships that takes into account the specific class position of Black women who are generally marginal in the labor force, while at this particular time some of us are temporarily viewed as doubly desirable tokens at white-collar and professional levels. We need to articulate the real class situation of persons who are not merely raceless, sexless workers, but for whom racial and sexual oppression are significant determinants in their working/economic lives. Although we are in essential agreement with Marx's theory as it applied to the very specific economic relationships he analyzed, we know that his analysis must be extended further in order for us to understand our specific economic situation as Black women.

A political contribution which we feel we have already made is the expansion of the feminist principle that the personal is political. In our consciousness-raising sessions, for example, we have in many ways gone beyond white women's revelations because we are dealing with the implications of race and class as well as sex. Even our Black women's style of talking/testifying in Black language about what we have experienced has a resonance that is both cultural and political. We have spent a great deal of energy delving into the cultural and experiential nature of our oppression out of necessity because none of these matters has ever been looked at before. No one before has ever examined the multilayered texture of Black women's lives. An example of this kind of revelation/conceptualization occurred at a meeting as we discussed the ways in which our early intellectual interests had been attacked by our peers, particularly Black males.

We discovered that all of us, because we were "smart" had also been considered "ugly," i.e., "smart-ugly." "Smart-ugly" crystallized the way in which most of us had been forced to develop our intellects at great cost to our "social" lives. The sanctions in the Black and white communities against Black women thinkers is comparatively much higher than for white women, particularly ones from the educated middle and upper classes.

As we have already stated, we reject the stance of Lesbian separatism because it is not a viable political analysis or strategy for us. It leaves out far too much and far too many people, particularly Black men, women, and children. We have a great deal of criticism and loathing for what men have been socialized to be in this society: what they support, how they act, and how they oppress. But we do not have the misguided notion that it is their maleness, per se—i.e., their biological maleness—that makes them what they are. As Black women we find any type of biological determinism a particularly dangerous and reactionary basis upon which to build a politic. We must also question whether Lesbian separatism is an adequate and progressive political analysis and strategy, even for those who practice it, since it so completely denies any but the sexual sources of women's oppression, negating the facts of class and race.

4 | WHERE DO SLAVERY AND COLONIALISM FIT?

Study Questions:

1. What two aspects of primitive accumulation does Marx identify, one within Europe and one in the colonies?
2. How can we fill in Marx's picture—what's missing, particularly *outside* Europe?
3. Where do we see primitive accumulation today?

Key Concepts:

– Primitive Accumulation: narrowly, the use of non-economic coercion, violence, force, and state policy to *jumpstart* early capitalist accumulation and *accelerate* the transition from feudalism to capitalism.

Karl Marx, *Capital, Vol. 1* (1867)

Chapter 26: The Secret of Primitive Accumulation

. . . the methods of primitive accumulation are anything but idyllic . . . so-called primitive accumulation, therefore, is nothing else than the historical process of divorcing the producer from the means of production. It appears as primitive, because it forms the prehistoric stage of capital and of the mode of production corresponding with it. The economic structure of capitalist society has grown out of the economic structure of feudal society. The dissolution of the latter set free the elements of the former.

The immediate producer, the laborer, could only dispose of his own person after he had ceased to be attached to the soil and ceased to be the slave, serf, or bondsman of another. To become a free seller of labor power, who carries his commodity wherever he finds a market, he must further have escaped from the regime of the guilds, their rules for apprentices and journeymen, and the impediments of their labor regulations. Hence, the historical movement which changes the producers into wage-workers, appears, on the one hand, as their emancipation from serfdom and from the fetters of the guilds, and this side alone exists for our bourgeois historians. But, on the other hand, these new freedmen became sellers of themselves only after they had been robbed of all their own means of production, and of all the guarantees of existence afforded by the old feudal arrangements. And the history of this, their expropriation, is written in the annals of mankind in letters of blood and fire.

Chapter 27: Expropriation of the Agricultural Population from the Land

The prelude of the revolution that laid the foundation of the capitalist mode of production, was played in the last third of the fifteenth, and the first decade of the sixteenth century. A mass of free proletarians was hurled on the labor market by the breaking-up of the bands of feudal retainers. . . . In insolent conflict with king and parliament, the great feudal lords created an incomparably larger proletariat by the forcible driving of the peasantry from the land, to which the latter had the same feudal right as the lord himself, and by the usurpation of the common lands. . . .

Communal property—always distinct from the State property just dealt with—was an old Teutonic institution which lived on under cover of feudalism. We have seen how the forcible usurpation of this, generally accompanied by the turning of arable into pasture-land, begins at the end of the fifteenth and extends into the sixteenth century. But, at that time, the process was carried on by means of individual acts of violence against which legislation, for a hundred and fifty years, fought in vain. The advance made by the eighteenth century shows itself in this, that the law itself becomes now the instrument of the theft of the people's land, although the large farmers make use of their little independent methods as well. The parliamentary form of the robbery is that of Acts for enclosures of Commons, in other words, decrees by which the landlords grant themselves the people's land as private property, decrees of expropriation of the people. . . .

Chapter 28: Bloody Legislation Against the Expropriated

The proletariat created by the breaking up of the bands of feudal retainers and by the forcible expropriation of the people from the soil, this "free" proletariat could not possibly be absorbed by the nascent manufactures as fast as it was thrown upon the world. On the other hand, these men, suddenly dragged from their wonted mode of life, could not as suddenly adapt themselves to the discipline of their new condition. They were turned *en masse* into beggars, robbers, vagabonds, partly from inclination, in most cases from stress of circumstances. Hence at the end of the fifteenth and during the whole of the sixteenth century, throughout Western Europe a bloody legislation against vagabondage. The fathers of the present working class were chastised for their enforced transformation into vagabonds and paupers. Legislation treated them as "voluntary" criminals, and assumed that it depended on their own good will to go on working under the old conditions that no longer existed.

In England this legislation began under Henry VII.

> Henry VIII. 1530: Beggars old and unable to work receive a beggar's license. On the other hand, whipping and imprisonment for sturdy vagabonds. They are to be tied to the cart-tail and whipped until the blood streams from their bodies. . . .
>
> Edward VI.: A statute of the first year of his reign, 1547, ordains that if anyone refuses to work, he shall be condemned as a slave to the person who has denounced him as an idler. The master shall feed his slave on bread and water, weak broth and such refuse meat as he thinks fit. He has the right to force him to do any work, no matter how disgusting, with whip and chains. If the slave is absent a fortnight, he is condemned to slavery for life and is to be branded on forehead or back with the letter S; if he runs away thrice, he is to be executed as a felon. The master can sell him, bequeath him, let him out on hire as a slave, just as any other personal chattel or cattle. If the slaves attempt anything against the masters, they are also to be executed. Justices of the peace, on information, are to hunt the rascals down. If it happens that a vagabond has been idling about for three days, he is to be taken to his birthplace, branded with a red-hot iron with the letter V on the breast and be set to work, in chains, in the streets or at some other labor. If the vagabond gives a false birthplace, he is then to become the slave for life of this place, of its inhabitants, or its corporation, and to be branded with an S.

> Elizabeth, 1572: Unlicensed beggars above 14 years of age are to be severely flogged and branded on the left ear unless some one will take them into service for two years; in case of a repetition of the offence, if they are over 18, they are to be executed. . . .
>
> James I: Any one wandering about and begging is declared a rogue and a vagabond. Justices of the peace in petty sessions are authorized to have them publicly whipped and for the first offence to imprison them. . . .

Thus were the agricultural people, first forcibly expropriated from the soil, driven from their homes, turned into vagabonds, and then whipped, branded, tortured by laws grotesquely terrible, into the discipline necessary for the wage system.

It is not enough that the conditions of labor are concentrated in a mass, in the shape of capital, at the one pole of society, while at the other are grouped masses of men, who have nothing to sell but their labor-power. Neither is it enough that they are compelled to sell it voluntarily. The advance of capitalist production develops a working class, which by education, tradition, habit, looks upon the conditions of that mode of production as self-evident laws of Nature. The organization of the capitalist process of production, once fully developed, breaks down all resistance. The constant generation of a relative surplus-population keeps the law of supply and demand of labor, and therefore keeps wages, in a rut that corresponds with the wants of capital. The dull compulsion of economic relations completes the subjection of the laborer to the capitalist. Direct force, outside economic conditions, is of course still used, but only exceptionally. In the ordinary run of things, the laborer can be left to the "natural laws of production," i.e., to his dependence on capital, a dependence springing from, and guaranteed in perpetuity by, the conditions of production themselves. It is otherwise during the historic genesis of capitalist production. The bourgeoisie, at its rise, wants and uses the power of the state to "regulate" wages, i.e., to force them within the limits suitable for surplus-value making, to lengthen the working-day and to keep the laborer himself in the normal degree of dependence. This is an essential element of the so-called primitive accumulation. . . .

Chapter 31: Genesis of the Industrial Capitalist

The genesis of the industrial capitalist did not proceed in such a gradual way as that of the farmer. Doubtless many small guild-masters, and yet more independent small artisans, or even wage laborers, transformed themselves into small capitalists, and (by gradually extending exploitation of wage labor and corresponding accumulation) into full-blown capitalists. In the infancy of capitalist production, things often happened as in the infancy of medieval towns, where the question, which of the escaped serfs should be master and which servant, was in great part decided by the earlier or later date of their flight. The snail's pace of this method corresponded in no wise with the commercial requirements of the new world market that the great discoveries of the end of the fifteenth century created. . . .

The discovery of gold and silver in America, the extirpation, enslavement and entombment in mines of the aboriginal population, the beginning of the conquest and looting of the East Indies, the turning of Africa into a warren for the commercial hunting of black-skins, signalized the rosy dawn of the era of capitalist production. These idyllic proceedings are the chief moments of primitive accumulation. . . . These methods depend in part on brute force, e.g., the colonial system. But, they all employ the power of the State, the concentrated and organized force of society, to hasten, hot-house fashion, the process of transformation of the feudal mode of production into the capitalist mode, and to shorten the transition. Force is the midwife of every old society pregnant with a new one. It is itself an economic power. . . .

Great fortunes sprang up like mushrooms in a day; primitive accumulation went on without the advance of a shilling. . . . The colonial system ripened, like a hot-house, trade and navigation. The "societies Monopolia" of Luther were powerful levers for concentration of capital. The colonies secured a market for the budding manufactures, and, through the monopoly of the market, an increased accumulation. The treasures captured outside Europe by undisguised looting, enslavement, and murder, floated back to the mother-country and were there turned into capital.

Whilst the cotton industry introduced child-slavery in England, it gave in the United States a stimulus to the transformation of the earlier, more or less patriarchal slavery, into a system of commercial exploitation. In fact, the veiled slavery of the wage workers in Europe needed, for its pedestal, slavery pure and simple in the new world.

Tantae molis erat, to establish the "eternal laws of Nature" of the capitalist mode of production, to complete the process of separation between laborers and conditions of labor, to transform, at one pole, the social means of production and subsistence into capital, at the opposite pole, the mass of the population into wage laborers, into "free laboring poor," that artificial product of modern society. If money, according to Augier, "comes into the world with a congenital blood-stain on one cheek," capital comes dripping from head to foot, from every pore, with blood and dirt.

Rosa Luxemburg, *The Accumulation of Capital* (1913)

Ch. 27—The Struggle against Natural Economy

Capitalism arises and develops historically amidst a non-capitalist society. In Western Europe it is found at first in a feudal environment from which it in fact sprang the system of bondage in rural areas and the guild system in the towns—and later, after having swallowed up the feudal system, it exists mainly in an environment of peasants and artisans, that is to say in a system of simple commodity production both in agriculture and trade. European capitalism is further surrounded by vast territories of non-European civilization ranging over all levels of development, from the primitive communist hordes of nomad herdsmen, hunters and gatherers to commodity production by peasants and artisans. This is the setting for the accumulation of capital.

We must distinguish three phases: the struggle of capital against natural economy, the struggle against commodity economy, and the competitive struggle of capital on the international stage for the remaining conditions of accumulation.

The existence and development of capitalism requires an environment of non-capitalist forms of production, but not every one of these forms will serve its ends. Capitalism needs non-capitalist social strata as a market for its surplus value, as a source of supply for its means of production and as a reservoir of labor power for its wage system. For all these purposes, forms of production based upon a natural economy are of no use to capital. In all social organizations where natural economy prevails, where there are primitive peasant communities with common ownership of the land, a feudal system of bondage or anything of this nature, economic organization is essentially in response to the internal demand; and therefore there is no demand, or very little, for foreign goods, and also, as a rule, no surplus production, or at least no urgent need to dispose of surplus products. What is most important, however, is that, in any natural economy, production only goes on because both means of production and labor power are bound in one form or another. . . . A natural economy thus confronts the requirements of capitalism at every turn with rigid barriers.

Capitalism must therefore always and everywhere fight a battle of annihilation against every historical form of natural economy that it encounters, whether this is slave economy, feudalism, primitive communism, or patriarchal peasant economy. The principal methods in this struggle are political force (revolution, war), oppressive taxation by the state, and cheap goods; they are partly applied simultaneously, and partly they succeed and complement one another. In Europe, force assumed revolutionary forms in the fight against feudalism (this is the ultimate explanation of the bourgeois revolutions in the seventeenth, eighteenth and nineteenth centuries); in the non-European countries, where it fights more primitive social organizations, it assumes the forms of colonial policy. . . .

In detail, capital in its struggle against societies with a natural economy pursues the following ends:

1. To gain immediate possession of important sources of productive forces such as land, game in primeval forests, minerals, precious stones and ores, products of exotic flora such as rubber, etc.
2. To 'liberate' labor power and to coerce it into service.
3. To introduce a commodity economy.
4. To separate trade and agriculture.

At the time of primitive accumulation, i.e. at the end of the Middle Ages, when the history of capitalism in Europe began, and right into the nineteenth century, dispossessing the peasants in England and on the Continent was the most striking weapon in the large-scale transformation of means of production and labor power into capital. Yet capital in power performs the same task even to-day, and on an even more important scale—by modern colonial policy.

It is an illusion to hope that capitalism will ever be content with the means of production which it can acquire by way of commodity exchange. In this respect already, capital is faced with difficulties because vast tracts of the globe's surface are in the possession of social organizations that have no desire for commodity exchange or cannot, because of the entire social structure and the forms of ownership, offer for sale the productive forces in which capital is primarily interested. The most important of these productive forces is of course the land, its hidden mineral treasure, and its meadows, woods and water, and further the flocks of the primitive shepherd tribes. If capital were here to rely on the process of slow internal disintegration, it might take centuries. . . .

Since the primitive associations of the natives are the strongest protection for their social organizations and for their material bases of existence, capital must begin by planning for the systematic destruction and annihilation of all the non-capitalist social units which obstruct its development. With that we have passed beyond the stage of primitive accumulation; this process is still going on. Each new colonial expansion is accompanied, as a matter of course, by a relentless battle of capital against the social and economic ties of the natives, who are also forcibly robbed of their means of production and labor power. . . .

Force is the only solution open to capital; the accumulation of capital, seen as an historical process, employs force as a permanent weapon, not only at its genesis, but further on down to the present day. From the point of view of the primitive societies involved, it is a matter of life or death; for them there can be no other attitude than opposition and fight to the finish—complete exhaustion and extinction. Hence permanent occupation of the colonies by the military, native risings and punitive expeditions are the order of the day for any colonial regime. The method of violence, then, is the immediate consequence of the clash between capitalism and the organizations of a natural economy which would restrict accumulation. . . . British policy in India and French policy in Algeria are the classical examples of the application of these methods by capitalism.

Angela Davis, "Reflections on the Black Woman's Role in the Community of Slaves" (1972)

If resistance was an organic ingredient of slave life, it had to be directly nurtured by the social organization which the slaves themselves improvised. The consciousness of their oppression, the conscious thrust towards its abolition could not have been sustained without impetus from the community they pulled together through the sheer force of their own strength. Of necessity, this community would revolve around the realm which was furthermost removed from the immediate arena of domination. It could only be located in and around the living quarters, the area where the basic needs of physical life were met.

In the area of production, the slaves—pressed into the mold of beasts of burden—were forcibly deprived of their humanity. (And a human being thoroughly dehumanized, has no desire for freedom.) But the community gravitating around the domestic quarters might possibly permit a retrieval of the man and the woman in their fundamental humanity. We can assume that in a very real material sense, it was only in domestic life—away from the eyes and whip of the overseer—that the slaves could attempt to assert the modicum of freedom they still retained. It was only there that they might be inspired to project techniques of expanding it further by leveling what few weapons they had against the slaveholding class whose unmitigated drive for profit was the source of their misery.

Via this path, we return to the African slave woman: in the living quarters, the major responsibilities "naturally" fell to her. It was the woman who was charged with keeping the "home" in order. This role was dictated by the male supremacist ideology of white society in America; it was also woven into the patriarchal traditions of Africa. As her biological destiny, the woman bore the fruits of procreation; as her social destiny, she cooked, sewed, washed, cleaned house, raised the children. Traditionally the labor of females, domestic work is supposed to complement and confirm their inferiority.

But with the black slave woman, there is a strange twist of affairs: in the infinite anguish of ministering to the needs of the men and children around her . . . she was performing the *only* labor of the slave community which could not be directly and immediately claimed by the oppressor. . . . Domestic labor was the only meaningful labor for the slave community as a whole. . . . Precisely through performing the drudgery which has long been the central expression of the socially conditioned inferiority of women, the black woman in chains could help to lay the foundation for some degree of autonomy, both for herself and for her men. Even as she was suffering under her unique oppression as female, she was thrust by the force of circumstances into the center of the slave community. She was, therefore, essential to the *survival* of the community. . . .

But much more remains to be said of the black woman during slavery. The dialectics of her oppression will become far more complex. This was one of the supreme ironies of slavery: in order to approach its strategic goal—to extract the greatest possible surplus from the labor of the slaves—the black woman had to be released from the chains of the myth of femininity. In the words of W.E.B. Du Bois, ". . . our women in black had freedom contemptuously thrust upon them." In order to function as slave, the black woman had to be annulled as woman. . . . The sheer force of things rendered her equal to her man. . . . She shared in the deformed equality of equal oppression.

But out of this deformed equality was forged quite undeliberately, yet inexorably, a state of affairs which could unharness an immense potential in the black woman. Expending indispensable labor for the enrichment of her oppressor, she could attain a practical awareness of the oppressor's utter dependence on her — for the master needs the slave far more than the slave needs the master. At the same time she could realize that while her productive activity was wholly subordinated to the will of the master, it was nevertheless proof of her ability to transform things. . . . The oppression of black women during the era of slavery, therefore, had to be buttressed by a level of overt ruling-class repression. Her routine oppression had to assume an unconcealed dimension of outright counter-insurgency. . . .

In confronting the black woman as adversary in a sexual contest, the master would be subjecting her to the most elemental form of terrorism distinctively suited for the female: rape. . . . In its political contours, the rape of the black woman was not exclusively an attack upon her. Indirectly, its target was also the slave community as a whole. In launching the sexual war on the woman, the master would not only assert his sovereignty over a critically important figure of the slave community, he would also be aiming a blow against the black man.

Robin D.G. Kelley, "Insecure: Policing Under Racial Capitalism" (2020)

According to data collected from the Ferguson Police Department between 2012 and 2014, African Americans accounted for 85 percent of vehicle stops, 90 percent of citations, and 93 percent of arrests, despite making up only 67 percent of the municipality's population. And yet, vehicle stops involving white drivers are far more likely to yield contraband than those involving African Americans. The proliferation of small municipalities in North St. Louis means that a Black driver can be ticketed by different officers passing through different jurisdiction, all on the same trip. If these fines or tickets are not paid, the court will issue arrest warrants, which may result in jail time or paying an inordinate sum to a bail bondsman, losing one's car or other property, or losing one's children to social services.

Summons and warrants are used as a kind of racial tax, an extraction of surplus directly by the state without producing anything besides discipline and terror and the reproduction of the state; in a word, revenue by primitive accumulation. In 2013, Ferguson's municipal court issued nearly 33,000 arrest warrants to a population of just over 21,000, generating about $2.6 million dollars in income for the municipality. That same year, the St. Louis County and City municipal courts acquired more than $61 million in fines and fees.

Where is the money coming from? Mostly from municipalities where, on average, 62 percent of the residents were Black and 22 percent lived below the poverty line. Elected officials, city bureaucrats and law enforcement worked tirelessly to squeeze as much money from poor vulnerable communities as possible. Just consider this passage from the US Department of Justice investigation into the Ferguson police department:

> City and police leadership pressure officers to write citations, independent of any public safety need, and rely on citation productivity to fund the City budget. In an email from March 2010, the Finance Director wrote to Chief [Thomas] Jackson that “unless ticket writing ramps up significantly before the end of the year, it will be hard to significantly raise collections next year. What are your thoughts? Given that we are looking at a substantial sales tax shortfall, it’s not an insignificant issue.” Chief Jackson responded that the City would see an increase in fines once more officers were hired and that he could target the $1.5 million forecast. Significantly, Chief Jackson stated that he was also “looking at different shift schedules which will place more officers on the street, which in turn will increase traffic enforcement per shift.”

5 | MANY PATHS TO SOCIALISM

Study Questions:

1. How did Marx change his view of historical development? Why did he change?
2. What happens when we begin to understand capitalism as a *global* system?
3. Do all societies *need* to pass through capitalism on the way to communism?

Key Concepts:

- Uneven Development: not a condition or an accident, but a *relationship* in which certain parts of the world "develop" by actively "underdeveloping" others through imperial control and the extraction of land, labor, and resources.
- Economic Dependency: a structural relation under global capitalism in which "peripheral" countries (which export low-value raw goods) exist in a relation of dependency to "core" countries (which export high-value manufactured goods).
- Global World-System: a view of the global capitalist system that distinguishes wealthy "core" (exploiter) countries from "peripheral" (exploited) countries, with the additional intermediate category of "semi-peripheral" countries (both exploiter and exploited).

Letter from Vera Zasulich to Karl Marx (February 16, 1881)

Honored Citizen,

You are not unaware that your *Capital* enjoys great popularity in Russia. Although the edition has been confiscated, the few remaining copies are read and re-read by the mass of more or less educated people in our country; serious men are studying it. What you probably do not realize is the role which your *Capital* plays in our discussions on the agrarian question in Russia and our rural commune. . . . But in my view, it is a life-and-death question above all for our socialist party. In one way or another, even the personal fate of our revolutionary socialists depends upon your answer to the question. For there are only two possibilities. Either the rural commune . . . is capable of developing in a socialist direction, that is, gradually organizing its production and distribution on a collectivist basis. In that case, the revolutionary socialist must devote all his strength to the liberation and development of the commune.

If, however, the commune is destined to perish, all that remains for the socialist, as such, is more or less ill-founded calculations as to how many decades it will take for the Russian peasant's land to pass into the hands of the bourgeoisie, and how many centuries it will take for capitalism in Russia to reach something like the level of development already attained in Western Europe. Their task will then be to conduct propaganda solely among the urban workers, while these workers will be continually drowned in the peasant mass which, following the dissolution of the commune, will be thrown on to the streets of the large towns in search of a wage.

Nowadays, we often hear it said that the rural commune is an archaic form condemned to perish by history, scientific socialism and, in short, everything above debate. Those who preach such a view call themselves your disciples par excellence: 'Marxists'. Their strongest argument is often: 'Marx said so'. . . . So you will understand, Citizen, how interested we are in your opinion. You would be doing us a very great favor if you were to set forth your ideas on the possible fate of our rural commune, and on the theory that it is historically necessary for every country in the world to pass through all the phases of capitalist production. . . .

With respectful greetings,
Vera Zasulich

Karl Marx: The reply to Zasulich (March 8, 1881) [the fifth and shortest draft]

Dear Citizen,

. . . I hope that a few lines will suffice to leave you in no doubt about the way in which my so-called theory has been misunderstood. In analyzing the genesis of capitalist production, I said:

> At the heart of the capitalist system is a complete separation of . . . the producer from the means of production . . . *the expropriation of the agricultural producer* is the basis of the whole process. Only in England has it been accomplished in a radical manner. . . . *But all the other countries of Western Europe* are following the same course.

The "historical inevitability" of this course is therefore *expressly* restricted to *the countries of Western Europe*. The reason for this restriction is indicated in Ch. XXXII: "*Private property*, founded upon personal labor . . . is supplanted by *capitalist private property*, which rests on exploitation of the labor of others, on wage labor."

In the Western case, then, *one form of private property is transformed into another form of private property*. In the case of the Russian peasants, however, *their communal property* would have to be transformed into private property.

The analysis in *Capital* therefore provides no reasons either for or against the vitality of the Russian commune. But the special study I have made of it, including a search for original source material, has convinced me that the commune is the fulcrum for social regeneration in Russia. But in order that it might function as such, the harmful influences assailing it on all sides must first be eliminated, and it must then be assured the normal conditions for spontaneous development.

I have the honor, dear Citizen, to remain, yours sincerely,

Karl Marx

José Carlos Mariátegui, *Seven Interpretive Essays on Peruvian Reality* (1927)

The degree to which the history of Peru was severed by the conquest can be seen better on an economic than on any other level. Here the conquest most clearly appears to be a break in continuity. Until the conquest, an economy developed in Peru that sprang spontaneously and freely from the Peruvian soil and people. The most interesting aspect of the empire of the Incas, which was a grouping of agricultural and sedentary communities, was its economy. All historical evidence agrees that the Inca people—industrious, disciplined, pantheist, and simple—lived in material comfort. With abundant food their population increased. . . . Collective work and common effort were employed fruitfully for social purposes.

The Spanish conquistadors destroyed this impressive productive machine without being able to replace it. The indigenous society and the Inca economy were wholly disrupted and annihilated by the shock of the conquest. Once the bonds that had united it were broken, the nation dissolved into scattered communities. Indigenous labor ceased to function as a concerted and integrated effort. The conquistadors were mainly concerned with distributing and wrangling over their rich booty. They plundered the treasures of temples and palaces; they allotted land and men with no thought of their future use as forces and means of production. . . .

Instead of making use of the Indian, he seemed to be intent on exterminating him. And the colonizers could not create a solid and integrated economy by themselves. . . . And since Negro slaves were imported to work on the coastal plantations, the elements and characteristics of a slave society were mixed into those of a feudal society. . . . These were the historical bases of the new Peruvian economy, of the colonial economy, colonial to its roots—a process that is still evolving. Let us now examine the outlines of a second stage, the stage in which a feudal economy gradually became a bourgeois economy, but without losing its colonial character within the world picture. . . .

I shall make a final observation: the elements of three different economies coexist in Peru today. Underneath the feudal economy inherited from the colonial period, vestiges of the indigenous communal economy can still be found in the sierra. On the coast, a bourgeois economy is growing in feudal soil; it gives every indication of being backward, at least in its mental outlook. . . .

The landowning class has not been transformed into a capitalist middle class, ally of the national economy. Mining, commerce, and transport are in the hands of foreign capital. The *latifundistas* [large landowners] have been satisfied to serve as the latter's intermediaries in the production of sugar and cotton. This economic system has kept agriculture to a semi-feudal organization that constitutes the heaviest burden on the country's development.

The survival of feudalism on the coast is reflected in the stagnation and poverty of urban life. There are few towns and cities on the coast, and the village as such hardly exists except for the occasional cluster of plots that still adorns the countryside in the midst of a feudalized agrarian structure. In Europe, the village is descended from the fief. On the Peruvian coast, the village does not exist because the fief is still preserved virtually intact. . . . Within European feudalism, the elements of growth—the factors of town life—were, in spite of the rural economy, much greater than within criollo semi-feudalism. . . .

The moral, political, and psychological elements of capitalism apparently have not found a favorable climate here. The capitalist, or rather the criollo landowner, believes in income before production. The love of adventure, the drive to create, and the organizing ability that characterize the authentic capitalist are almost unknown in Peru. . . .

The problem of the Indian is rooted in the land tenure system of our economy. Any attempt to solve it with administrative or police measures, through education or by a road building program, is superficial and secondary as long as the feudalism of the *gamonales* continues to exist. . . .

The agrarian problem is first and foremost the problem of eliminating feudalism in Peru, which should have been done by the democratic-bourgeois regime that followed the War of Independence. But in its one hundred years as a republic, Peru has not had a genuine bourgeois class, a true capitalist class. The old feudal class—camouflaged or disguised as a republican bourgeoisie—has kept its position. . . . There are two expressions of feudalism that survive: the latifundium and servitude.

Inseparable and of the same substance, their analysis leads us to the conclusion that the servitude oppressing the indigenous race cannot be abolished unless the latifundium is abolished. . . . In keeping with my ideological position, I believe that the moment for attempting the liberal, individualist method in Peru has already passed. Aside from reasons of doctrine, I consider that our agrarian problem has a special character due to an indisputable and concrete factor: the survival of the Indian "community" and of elements of practical socialism in indigenous agriculture and life.

Inca communism, which cannot be negated or disparaged for having developed under the autocratic regime of the Incas, is therefore designated as agrarian communism. The essential traits of the Inca economy . . . were the following:

> Collective ownership of farmland by the ayllu or group of related families, although the property was divided into individual and non-transferable lots; collective ownership of waters, pasture, and woodlands by the *marca* or tribe, or the federation of *ayllus* settled around a village; cooperative labor; individual allotment of harvests and produce.

Colonization unquestionably must bear the responsibility for the disappearance of this economy, together with the culture it nourished, not because it destroyed autochthonous forms but because it brought no superior substitutes. The colonial regime disrupted and demolished the Inca agrarian economy without replacing it with an economy of higher yields. Under the indigenous aristocracy, the natives made up a nation of ten million men, with an integrated government that efficiently ruled all its territory; under a foreign aristocracy, the natives became a scattered and anarchic mass of a million men reduced to servitude and peonage.

In this respect, demographic data are the most convincing and decisive. Although the Inca regime may be censured in the name of modern liberal concepts of liberty and justice, the positive and material historical fact is that it assured the subsistence and growth of a population that came to ten million when the conquistadors arrived in Peru, and that this population after three centuries of Spanish domination had fallen to one million. Colonization stands condemned not from any abstract, theoretical, or moral standpoint of justice, but from the practical, concrete, and material standpoint of utility. Colonization, failing to organize even a feudal economy in Peru, introduced elements of a slave economy. . . .

The Indian, in spite of one hundred years of republican legislation, has not become an individualist. And this is not because he resists progress, as is claimed by his detractors. Rather, it is because individualism under a feudal system does not find the necessary conditions to gain strength and develop. On the other hand, communism has continued to be the Indian's only defense. Individualism cannot flourish or even exist effectively outside a system of free competition. And the Indian has never felt less free than when he has felt alone.

Therefore, in Indian villages where families are grouped together that have lost the bonds of their ancestral heritage and community work, hardy and stubborn habits of cooperation and solidarity still survive that are the empirical expression of a Communist spirit. The "community" is the instrument of this spirit. When expropriation and redistribution seem about to liquidate the "community," indigenous socialism always finds a way to reject, resist, or evade this incursion.

Walter Rodney, *How Europe Underdeveloped Africa* (1972)

The notions of revolution and class consciousness must be borne in mind when it comes to examining the situation of the modern worker and peasant classes in Africa. However, for the greater part of Africa's history, the existing classes have been incompletely crystallized and the changes have been gradual rather than revolutionary. What is probably of more relevance for early African development is the principle that development over the world's territories has always been *uneven*. . . .

The fact that capitalism today is still around alongside of socialism should warn us that the modes of production cannot simply be viewed as a question of successive stages. Uneven development has always ensured that societies have come into contact when they were at different levels—for example, one that was communal and one that was capitalist. When two societies of different sorts come into prolonged and effective contact, the rate and character of change taking place in both is seriously affected to the extent that entirely new patterns are created. Two general rules can be observed to apply in such cases. Firstly, the weaker of the two societies (i.e., the one with less economic capacity) is bound to be adversely affected—and the bigger the gap between the two societies concerned the more detrimental are the consequences. For example, when European capitalism came into contact with the indigenous hunting societies of America and the Caribbean, the latter were virtually exterminated.

The African continent reveals very fully the workings of the law of uneven development of societies. There are marked contrasts between the Ethiopian empire and the hunting groups of pigmies in the Congo forest or between empires of the Western Sudan and the Khoisan hunter-gatherers of the Kalahari Desert. Indeed, there were striking contrasts within any given geographical area. The Ethiopian empire embraced literate feudal Amharic noblemen as well as simple Kaffa cultivators and Galla pastoralists. The empires of the Western Sudan had sophisticated, educated Mandinga townsmen, small communities of Bozo fishermen and nomadic Fulani herdsmen. Even among clans and lineages that appear roughly similar, there were considerable differences.

Both Marxists and non-Marxists alike (with different motivations) have pointed out that the sequence of modes of production noted in Europe were not reproduced in Africa. In Africa, after the communal stage there was no epoch of slavery arising out of internal evolution. Nor was there a mode of production which was the replica of European feudalism. Marx himself recognized that the stages of development in Asia had produced a form of society which could not easily be fitted into a European slot. That he called "the Asian mode of production." Following along those lines, a number of Marxists have recently been discussing whether Africa was in the same category as Asia or whether Africa has its own "African mode of production." The implications of the arguments are very progressive, because they are concerned with the concrete conditions of Africa rather than with preconceptions brought from Europe. But the scholars concerned seem to be bent on finding a single term to cover a variety of social formations which were existing in Africa from about the fifth century A.D. to the coming of colonialism. The assumption that will underlie this study is that most African societies before 1500 were in a transitional stage between the practice of agriculture (plus fishing and herding) in family communities and the practice of the same activities within states and societies comparable to feudalism. . . .

In the centuries before colonial rule, Europe increased its economic capacity by leaps and bounds, while Africa appeared to have been almost static. Africa in the late nineteenth century could still be described as part communal and part feudal, although Western Europe had moved completely from feudalism to capitalism. To elucidate the main thesis of this study, it is necessary to follow not only the development of Europe and the underdevelopment of Africa, but also to understand how those two combined in a single system—that of *capitalist imperialism* . . . what was a slight difference when the Portuguese sailed to West Africa in 1444 was a huge gap by the time that European robber statesmen sat down in Berlin 440 years later to decide who should steal which parts of Africa. It was that gap which provided both the necessity and the opportunity for Europe to move into the imperialist epoch, and to colonize and further underdevelop Africa.

6 | *BLACK RECONSTRUCTION*, PART I

Study Questions:

1. Why does Du Bois call his chapters "The Black Worker" and "The White Worker"?
2. Why does he speak of "The General Strike" and what does he mean by this?
3. Was the Civil War about slavery? Yes or no.
4. Who freed the slaves? Who won the Civil War?

Key Concepts:

- The Black Worker: *all* laborers who are Black, North and South, enslaved and free.
- The White Worker: *all* laborers who are white, North and South, rural and industrial.
- The General Strike: the period beginning in 1861 when five hundred thousand Black workers left southern plantations en masse and congregated in mass camps around the Union Army, with many helping the northern war effort as spies, scouts, and soldiers.

Timeline:

- 1850—Fugitive Slave Act is passed by Congress.
- 1859, October—John Brown's raid on Harper's Ferry.

- 1860, November—Lincoln is elected.
- 1861, February—Seven lower southern states secede.
- 1861, April—War breaks out at Fort Sumter.
- 1862—Black soldiers are recruited to Union forces on the South Carolina Sea Islands.
- 1863, January—Lincoln issues the Emancipation Proclamation.
- 1864, November—Lincoln is reelected.
- 1865, January—Thirteenth Amendment is approved. General Sherman issues Field Order Number 15, authorizing freed Black people to seize lands.
- 1865, April—War ends, Lincoln is assassinated, Reconstruction begins.

W.E.B. Du Bois—*Black Reconstruction in America* (1935)

Chapter I. The Black Worker

Black labor became the foundation stone not only of the Southern social structure, but of Northern manufacture and commerce, of the English factory system, of European commerce, of buying and selling on a world-wide scale; new cities were built on the results of black labor, and a new labor problem, involving all white labor, arose both in Europe and America. . . .

The system of slavery demanded a special police force and such a force was made possible and unusually effective by the presence of the poor whites. This explains the difference between the slave revolts in the West Indies, and the lack of effective revolt in the Southern United States. In the West Indies, the power over the slave was held by the whites and carried out by them and such Negroes as they could trust. In the South, on the other hand, the great planters formed proportionately quite as small a class but they had singularly enough at their command some five million poor whites; that is, there were actually more white people to police the slaves than there were slaves. Considering the economic rivalry of the black and white worker in the North, it would have seemed natural that the poor white would have refused to police the slaves. But two considerations led him in the opposite direction. First of all, it gave him work and some authority as overseer, slave driver, and member of the patrol system. But above and beyond this, it fed his vanity because it associated him with the masters. Slavery bred in the poor white a dislike of Negro toil of all sorts. He never regarded himself as a laborer, or as part of any labor movement. If he had any ambition at all it was to become a planter and to own "niggers." To these Negroes he transferred all the dislike and hatred which he had for the whole slave system. The result was that the system was held stable and intact by the poor white. Even with the late ruin of Haiti before their eyes, the planters, stirred as they were, were nevertheless able to stamp out slave revolt. The dozen revolts of the eighteenth century had dwindled to the plot of Gabriel in 1800, Vesey in 1822, of Nat Turner in 1831 and crews of the Amistad and Creole in 1839 and 1841. Gradually the whole white South became an armed and commissioned camp to keep Negroes in slavery and to kill the black rebel. . . .

The true significance of slavery in the United States to the whole social development of America lay in the ultimate relation of slaves to democracy. What were to be the limits of democratic control in the United States? If all labor, black as well as white, became free—were given schools and the right to vote—what control could or should be set to the power and action of these laborers? Was the rule of the mass of Americans to be unlimited, and the right to rule extended to all men regardless of race and color, or if not, what power of dictatorship and control; and how would property and privilege be protected? This was the great and primary question which was in the minds of the men who wrote the Constitution of the United States and continued in the minds of thinkers down through the slavery controversy. It still remains with the world as the problem of democracy expands and touches all races and nations. . . .

Above all, we must remember the black worker was the ultimate exploited; that he formed that mass of labor which had neither wish nor power to escape from the labor status, in order to directly exploit other laborers, or indirectly, by alliance with capital, to share in their exploitation. . . . It was thus the black worker, as founding stone of a new economic system in the nineteenth century and for the modern world, who brought civil war in America. He was its underlying cause, in spite of every effort to base the strife upon union and national power. That dark and vast sea of human labor in China and India, the South Seas and all Africa; in the West Indies and Central America and in the United States—that great majority of mankind, on whose bent and broken backs rest today the founding stones of modern industry—shares a common destiny; it is despised and rejected by race and color; paid a wage below the level of decent living; driven, beaten, prisoned and enslaved in all but name; spawning the world's raw material and luxury—cotton, wool, coffee, tea, cocoa, palm oil, fibers, spices, rubber, silks, lumber, copper, gold, diamonds, leather—how shall we end the list and where? . . .

Here is the real modern labor problem. Here is the kernel of the problem of Religion and Democracy, of Humanity. Words and futile gestures avail nothing. Out of the exploitation of the dark proletariat comes the Surplus Value filched from human beasts which, in cultured lands, the Machine and harnessed Power veil and conceal. The emancipation of man is the emancipation of labor and the emancipation of labor is the freeing of that basic majority of workers who are yellow, brown and black. . . .

Chapter II. The White Worker

These workers came to oppose slavery not so much from moral as from the economic fear of being reduced by competition to the level of slaves. They wanted a chance to become capitalists; and they found that chance threatened by the competition of a working class whose status at the bottom of the economic structure seemed permanent and inescapable. . . . In Philadelphia, 1828–1840, a series of riots took place which thereafter extended until after the Civil War. The riot of 1834 took the dimensions of a pitched battle and lasted for three days. Thirty-one houses and two churches were destroyed. Other riots took place in 1835 and 1838 and a two days' riot in 1842 caused the calling out of the militia with artilllery. . . . What they failed to comprehend was that the black man enslaved was an even more formidable and fatal competitor than the black man free . . . this competition was present and would continue and would be emphasized if the Negro continued as a slave worker. . . .

In all this consideration, we have so far ignored the white workers of the South and we have done this because the labor movement ignored them and the abolitionists ignored them; and above all, they were ignored by Northern capitalists and Southern planters. They were in many respects almost a forgotten mass of men. Cairnes describes the slave South, the period just before the war:

> It resolves itself into three classes, broadly distinguished from each other, and connected by no common interest—the slaves on whom devolves all the regular industry, the slaveholders who reap all its fruits, and an idle and lawless rabble who live dispersed over vast plains in a condition little removed from absolute barbarism.

While revolt against the domination of the planters over the poor whites was voiced by men like Helper, who called for a class struggle to destroy the planters, this was nullified by deep-rooted antagonism to the Negro, whether slave or free. If black labor could be expelled from the United States or eventually exterminated, then the fight against the planter could take place. But the poor whites and their leaders could not for a moment contemplate a fight of united white and black labor against the exploiters. Indeed, the natural leaders of the poor whites, the small farmer, the merchant, the professional man, the white mechanic and slave overseer, were bound to the planters and repelled from the slaves and even from the mass of the white laborers in two ways: first, they constituted the police patrol who could ride with planters and now and then exercise unlimited force upon recalcitrant or runaway slaves; and then, too, there was always a chance that they themselves might also become planters by saving money, by investment, by the power of good luck; and the only heaven that attracted them was the life of the great Southern planter. . . .

America thus stepped forward in the first blossoming of the modern age and added to the Art of Beauty, gift of the Renaissance, and to Freedom of Belief, gift of Martin Luther and Leo X, a vision of democratic self-government: the domination of political life by the intelligent decision of free and self-sustaining men. . . . And then some unjust God leaned, laughing, over the ramparts of heaven and dropped a black man in the midst. It transformed the world. It turned democracy back to Roman Imperialism and Fascism; it restored caste and oligarchy; it replaced freedom with slavery and withdrew the name of humanity from the vast majority of human beings.

But not without struggle. . . . Then came this battle called Civil War, beginning in Kansas in 1854, and ending in the presidential election of 1876—twenty awful years. The slave went free; stood a brief moment in the sun; then moved back again toward slavery. The whole weight of America was thrown to color caste. The colored world went down before England, France, Germany, Russia, Italy and America. A new slavery arose. The upward moving of white labor was betrayed into wars for profit based on color caste. Democracy died save in the hearts of black folk. Indeed, the plight of the white working class throughout the world today is directly traceable to Negro slavery in America. . . .

Chapter IV. The General Strike

When Edwin Ruffin, white-haired and mad, fired the first gun at Fort Sumter, he freed the slaves. It was the last thing he meant to do but that was because he was so typically a Southern oligarch. He did not know the real world about him. . . . Outside of agriculture, he jumped at conclusions instead of testing them by careful research. He knew, for instance, that the North would not fight. He knew that Negroes would never revolt.

And so war came. . . . When Northern armies entered the South they became armies of emancipation. It was the last thing they planned to be. The North did not propose to attack property. It did not propose to free slaves. This was to be a white man's war to preserve the Union, and the Union must be preserved. Nothing that concerned the amelioration of the Negro touched the heart of the mass of Americans nor could the common run of men realize the political and economic cost of Negro slavery. . . . Negroes on the whole were considered cowards and inferior beings whose very presence in America was unfortunate. The abolitionists, it was true, expected action on the part of the Negro, but how much, they could not say. Only John Brown knew just how revolt had come and would come and he was dead. . . .

It must be borne in mind that nine-tenths of the four million black slaves could neither read nor write, and that the overwhelming majority of them were isolated on country plantations. Any mass movement under such circumstances must materialize slowly and painfully. What the Negro did was to wait, look and listen and try to see where his interest lay. There was no use in seeking refuge in an army which was not an army of freedom; and there was no sense in revolting against armed masters who were conquering the world. As soon, however, as it became clear that the Union armies would not or could not return fugitive slaves, and that the masters with all their fume and fury were uncertain of victory, the slave entered upon a general strike against slavery by the same methods that he had used during the period of the fugitive slave. He ran away to the first place of safety and offered his services to the Federal Army. So that in this way it was really true that he served his former master and served the emancipating army; and it was also true that this withdrawal and bestowal of his labor decided the war.

The South counted on Negroes as laborers to raise food and money crops for civilians and for the army, and even in a crisis, to be used for military purposes. . . . This was not merely the desire to stop work. It was a strike on a wide basis against the conditions of work. It was a general strike that involved directly in the end perhaps a half million people. They wanted to stop the economy of the plantation system, and to do that they left the plantations. . . . But this slow, stubborn mutiny of the Negro slave was not merely a matter of 200,000 black soldiers and perhaps 300,000 other black laborers, servants, spies and helpers. Back of this half million stood 3 ½ million more. Without their labor the South would starve. With arms in their hands, Negroes would form a fighting force which could replace every single Northern white soldier fighting listlessly and against his will with a black man fighting for freedom. . . .

The slave, despite every effort, was becoming the center of war. Lincoln, with his uncanny insight, began to see it. He began to talk about compensation for emancipated slaves, and Congress, following almost too quickly, passed the Confiscation Act in August 1861, freeing slaves which were actually used in war by the enemy. Lincoln then suggested that provision be made for colonization of such slaves. He simply could not envisage free Negroes in the United States. What would become of them? What would they do? . . . The war was not to abolish slavery, and if Lincoln could hold the country together and keep slavery, he would do it.

But he could not, and he had no sooner said this than he began to realize that he could not. In June, 1862, slavery was abolished in the territories. . . . Lincoln faced the truth, front forward; and that truth was not simply that Negroes ought to be free; it was that thousands of them were already free, and that either the power which slaves put into the hands of the South was to be taken from it, or the North could not win the war. Either the Negro was to be allowed to fight, or the draft itself would not bring enough white men into the army to keep up the war. . . .

Chapter V. The Coming of the Lord

. . . In December, 1863, Morgan led Negro troops in the battle of Nashville. He declared a new chapter in the history of liberty had been written. "It had been shown that marching under a flag of freedom, animated by a love of liberty, even the slave becomes a man and a hero." Between eight and ten thousand Negro troops took part in the battles around Nashville, all of them from slave states.

When General Thomas rode over the battlefield, and saw the bodies of colored men side by side with the foremost on the very works of the enemy, he turned to his staff, saying: "Gentlemen, the question is settled: Negroes will fight."

How extraordinary, and what a tribute to ignorance and religious hypocrisy, is the fact that in the minds of most people, even those of liberals, only murder makes men. The slave pleaded; he was humble; he protected the women of the South, and the world ignored him. The slave killed white men; and behold, he was a man! . . .

And yet emancipation came not simply to black folk in 1863; to white Americans came slowly a new vision and a new uplift, a sudden freeing of hateful mental shadows. At last democracy was to be justified of its own children. The nation was to be purged of continual sin not indeed all of its own doing—due partly to its inheritance; and yet a sin, a negation that gave the world the right to sneer at the pretensions of this republic. At last there could really be a free commonwealth of freemen. Thus, amid enthusiasm and philanthropy, and religious fervor that surged over the whole country, the black man became in word "henceforward and forever free."

7 | *BLACK RECONSTRUCTION*, PART II

Study Questions:

1. Who benefited from Reconstruction? Name specific groups but also think broadly.
2. How and why did Reconstruction come to an end?
3. What were the *international* consequences of Reconstruction's defeat?
4. What did Du Bois mean when he said former slaves moved "back toward slavery"?

Key Concepts:

– Abolition-Democracy: the movement to abolish slavery and expand democracy to formerly enslaved people and the *kind* of democracy—and society—that becomes possible when slavery and white supremacy are in retreat.

Timeline:

- 1865, April—Lincoln is assassinated and replaced by Andrew Johnson; war ends and Reconstruction begins; Ku Klux Klan is created in Tennessee.
- 1866—Fourteenth Amendment approved citizenship; Race riots/massacres in Memphis (May) and New Orleans (July).

- 1867—Reconstruction Acts are approved by Congress over Johnson's veto.
- 1868—Fourteenth Amendment ratified as a condition for southern states' reentry into the Union; Ulysses S. Grant is elected president, but provides no strong support for Reconstruction.
- 1869—Fifteenth Amendment (voting rights) is approved.
- 1871—US government no longer recognizes Indigenous sovereignty and begins to confiscate Native land.
- 1868–1877—Radical Reconstruction, including a Black majority South Carolina.
- 1873–1875—Nationwide recession weakens Republican support for reconstruction.
- 1877—Compromise of 1877 gives Rutherford B. Hayes the presidency in exchange for withdrawing troops from the South and ending Reconstruction.
- 1880–1900—Black sharecroppers are displaced and indebted; Black Codes expand; Black voting rights are wiped out across the South; emergence of convict leasing, policing, and Jim Crow segregation.

W.E.B. Du Bois—*Black Reconstruction in America* (1935)

Chapter VI. Looking Backward

As the Civil War staggered toward its end, the country began to realize that it was not only at the end of an era, but it was facing the beginning of a vaster and more important cycle. The emancipation of four million slaves might end slavery, but would it not also be the end of its four million victims? To be sure there were many prophets, South and North, who foretold this fate of Negro extinction, but they were wrong. It was the beginning of Negro development, and what was this development going to be? . . . The answers to this problem, historically, had taken these forms:

1. Negroes, after conversion to Christianity, were in the same position as other colonial subjects of the British King. This attitude disappeared early in colonial history.
2. When the slave trade was stopped, Negroes would die out. Therefore, the attack upon slavery must begin with the abolition of the slave trade and after that the race problem would settle itself. This attitude was back of the slave trade laws, 1808–20.
3. If Negroes did not die out, and if gradually by emancipation and the economic failure of slavery they became free, they must be systematically deported out of the country, back to Africa or elsewhere, where they would develop into an independent people or die from laziness or disease. This represented the attitude of liberal America from the end of the War of 1812 down to the beginning of the Cotton Kingdom.
4. Negroes were destined to be perpetual slaves in a new economy which recognized a caste of slave workers. And this caste system might eventually displace the white worker. At any rate, it was destined to wider expansion toward the tropics. This was the attitude of the Confederacy.

It is clear that from the time of Washington and Jefferson down to the Civil War, when the nation was asked if it was possible for free Negroes to become American citizens in the full sense of the word, it answered by a stern and determined "No!" The persons who conceived of the Negroes as free and remaining in the United States were a small minority before 1861, and confined to educated free Negroes and some of the Abolitionists. . . .

As late as April, 1865, President Lincoln said to General Butler:

> "But what shall we do with the Negroes after they are free?" inquired Lincoln. "I can hardly believe that the South and North can live in peace unless we get rid of the Negroes. Certainly they cannot, if we don't get rid of the Negroes whom we have armed and disciplined and who have fought with us, to the amount, I believe, of some 150,000 men. I believe that it would be better to export them all to some fertile country with a good climate, which they could have to themselves. . . . Now we shall have no use for our very large navy. What then are our difficulties in sending the blacks away?"

Chapter VII. Looking Forward

. . . two quite distinct but persistently undifferentiated visions of the future dominated the triumphant North after the war. One was the prolongation of Puritan idealism, transformed by the frontier into a theory of universal democracy, and now expressed by Abolitionists . . . together with some of the leaders of the new labor movement. The other trend was entirely different and is confused with the democratic ideal because the two ideals lay confused in so many individual minds. This was the development of industry in America and of a new industrial philosophy.

The new industry had a vision not of work but of wealth; not of planned accomplishment, but of power. It became the most conscienceless, unmoral system of industry which the world has experienced. It went with ruthless indifference towards waste, death, ugliness and disaster, and yet reared the most stupendous machine for the efficient organization of work which the world has ever seen. . . . Behind this extraordinary industrial development, as justification in the minds of men, lay what we may call the great

American Assumption, which up to the time of the Civil War, was held more or less explicitly by practically all Americans. The American Assumption was that wealth is mainly the result of its owner's effort and that any average worker can by thrift become a capitalist. The curious thing about this assumption was that . . . it was not true. . . .

The abolition-democracy was the liberal movement among both laborers and small capitalists, who united in the American Assumption, but saw the danger of slavery to both capital and labor. It began its moral fight against slavery in the thirties and forties and, gradually transformed by economic elements, concluded it during the war. The object and only real object of the Civil War in its eyes was the abolition of slavery, and it was convinced that this could be thoroughly accomplished only if the emancipated Negroes became free citizens and voters. . . . Thus abolition-democracy was pushed towards the conception of a dictatorship of labor, although few of its advocates wholly grasped the fact that this necessarily involved dictatorship by labor over capital and industry. . . .

Negroes deserved not only the pity of the world but the gratitude of both South and North. Under extraordinary provocation they had acted like decent human beings. . . . Yet after the war they were still not free; they were still practically slaves, and how was their freedom to be made a fact? It could be done in only one way. They must have the protection of law; and back of law must stand physical force. They must have land; they must have education. How was all this to be done? . . .

Chapter IX. The Price of Disaster

The price of the disaster of slavery and civil war was the necessity of quickly assimilating into American democracy a mass of ignorant laborers in whose hands alone for the moment lay the power of preserving the ideals of popular government; of overthrowing a slave economy and establishing upon it an industry primarily for the profit of the workers. It was this price which in the end America refused to pay and today suffers for that refusal. . . .

The Abolitionists were not enemies of capital. . . . But the former Abolitionists were gradually developing. Under the leadership of Stevens and Sumner, they were beginning to realize the economic foundation of the revolution necessary in the South. They saw that the Negro needed land and education and that his vote would only be valuable to him as it opened the doors to a firm economic foundation and real intelligence. If now they could get the industrial North, not simply to give the Negro the vote, but to give him land and give him schools, the battle would be won. Here, however, they were only partially successful. . . .

It was a dictatorship backed by the military arm of the United States by which the governments of the Southern states were to be coerced into accepting a new form of administration, in which the freedmen and the poor whites were to hold the overwhelming balance of political power. As soon as political power was successfully delivered into the hands of these elements, the Federal government was to withdraw and full democracy ensue. The difficulty with this theory was the failure to realize that such dictatorship must last long enough really to put the mass of workers in power; that this would be in fact a dictatorship of the proletariat which must endure until the proletariat or at least a leading united group, with clear objects and effective method, had education and experience and had taken firm control of the economic organization of the South. Unfortunately, the power set to begin this dictatorship was the military arm of a government which more and more was falling into the hands of organized wealth, and of wealth organized on a scale never before seen in modern civilization. . . .

It was inconceivable, therefore, that the masters of Northern industry through their growing control of American government, were going to allow the laborers of the South any more real control of wealth and industry than was necessary to curb the political power of the planters and their successors. As soon as the Southern landholders and merchants yielded to the Northern demands of a plutocracy, at that moment the military dictatorship should be withdrawn and a dictatorship of capital allowed unhampered sway. . . .

As the Negro laborers organized separately, there came slowly to realization the fact that here was not only separate organization but a separation in leading ideas; because among Negroes, and particularly in the South, there was being put into force one of the most extraordinary experiments of Marxism that the world, before the Russian revolution, had seen. That is, backed by the military power of the United States, a dictatorship of labor was to be attempted and those who were leading the Negro race in this vast experiment were emphasizing the necessity of the political power and organization backed by protective military power. On the other hand, the trade union movement of the white labor in the North was moving away from that idea and moving away from politics. They seemed to see a more purely economic solution in their demand for higher wages and shorter hours. . . .

As the Negroes moved from unionism toward political action, white labor in the North not only moved in the opposite direction from political action to union organization, but also evolved the American Blindspot for the Negro and his problems. It lost interest and vital touch with Southern labor and acted as though the millions of laborers in the South did not exist.

Thus labor went into the great war of 1877 against Northern capitalists unsupported by the black man, and the black man went his way in the South to strengthen and consolidate his power, unsupported by Northern labor. Suppose for a moment that Northern labor had stopped the bargain of 1876 and maintained the power of the labor vote in the South; and suppose that the Negro with new and dawning consciousness of the demands of labor as differentiated from the demands of capitalists, had used his vote more specifically for the benefit of white labor. . . .

Chapter X. The Black Proletariat in South Carolina

We rule by junta; we turn Fascist, because we do not believe in men; yet the basis of fact in this disbelief is incredibly narrow. We know perfectly well that most human beings have never had a decent human chance to be full men. Most of us may be convinced that even with opportunity the number of utter human failures would be vast; and yet remember that this assumption kept the ancestors of present white America long in slavery and degradation. It is then one's moral duty to see that every human being, to the extent of his capacity, escapes ignorance, poverty and crime. With this high ideal held unswervingly in view, monarchy, oligarchy, dictatorships may rule; but the end will be the rule of All, if mayhap All or Most qualify. The only unforgivable sin is dictatorship for the benefit of Fools, Voluptuaries, gilded Satraps, Prostitutes and Idiots. The rule of the famished, unlettered, stinking mob is better than this and the only inevitable, logical and justifiable return. . . .

The contention attacked race discrimination squarely. . . . Thus, discriminations of race and color were abolished by the constitution, and practical application was attempted in the case of the public schools, and the militia. The convention framed the most liberal provisions for the right of suffrage that any of the Southern constitutions provided. They did not attempt, as in Virginia, Alabama, and Mississippi, to restrict the voting of whites further than was provided by the Reconstruction acts. . . . Of course, they made no distinction in race and color. The rights of women were enlarged. The property of married women could not be sold for their husbands' debts, and for the first time in its history, the state was given a divorce law.

Education was discussed at length, and a free common school system voted for. . . . Among other things, the constitution abolished imprisonment for debt, and dueling, and did away with property qualifications, for voting or holding office . . . an orphan asylum was authorized in 1869, the poor of the state were provided for in 1870; and this system was kept after the whites came into power. An institution for the deaf, dumb and blind was started in 1871. It lasted until 1873, and then the faculty resigned because they were ordered to accept colored students. A lunatic asylum was provided and colored patients admitted. . . .

Beneath the race issue, and unconsciously of more fundamental weight, was the economic issue. Men were seeking again to reestablish the domination of property in Southern politics. By getting rid of the black labor vote, they would take their first and substantial step. By raising the race issue, they would secure domination over the white labor vote, and thus the oligarchy that ruled the South before the war would be in part restored to power. . . .

Chapter XIV. Counter-Revolution of Property

. . . eagerness on the part of the poor whites to check the demands of the Negroes by any means, and by willingness to do the dirty work of the revolution that was coming, with its blood and crass cruelties, its bitter words, upheaval and turmoil. This was the birth and being of the Ku Klux Klan. . . . The white South, therefore, quickly substituted violence and renewal of the war in order to get rid of the possibility of good government supported by black labor votes. . . .

Thus, both the liberal and the conservative North found themselves willing to sacrifice the interests of labor in the South to the interest of capital. The temporary dictatorship as represented by the Freedmen's Bureau was practically ended by 1870. This led to an increase of violence on the part of the Ku Klux Klan to subject black labor to strict domination by capital and to break Negro political power. . . .

The military dictatorship was withdrawn, and the representatives of Northern capital gave up all efforts to lead the Negro vote. The new dictatorship became a manipulation of the white labor vote which followed the lines of similar control in the North, while it proceeded to deprive the black voter by violence and force of any vote at all. The rivalry of these two classes of labor and their competition neutralized the labor vote in the South. The black voter struggled and appealed, but it was in vain. And the United States, reenforced by the increased political power of the South based on disfranchisement of black voters, took its place to reenforce the capitalistic dictatorship of the United States, which became the most powerful in the world, and which backed the new industrial imperialism and degraded colored labor the world over.

This meant a tremendous change in the whole intellectual and spiritual development of civilization in the South and in the United States because of the predominant political power of the South, built on disfranchised labor. The United States was turned into a reactionary force. It became the cornerstone of that new imperialism which is subjecting the labor of yellow, brown and black peoples to the dictation of capitalism organized on a world basis; and it has not only brought nearer the revolution by which the power of capitalism is to be challenged, but also it is transforming the fight to the sinister aspect of a fight on racial lines embittered by awful memories. . . .

God wept; but that mattered little to an unbelieving age; what mattered most was that the world wept and still is weeping and blind with tears and blood. For there began to rise in America in 1876 a new capitalism and a new enslavement of labor. . . . Sons of ditch-diggers aspired to be spawn of bastard kings and thieving aristocrats rather than of rough-handed children of dirt and toil. The immense profit from this new exploitation and world-wide commerce enabled a guild of millionaires to engage the greatest engineers, the wisest men of science, as well as pay high wage to the more intelligent labor and at the same time to have left enough surplus to make more thorough the dictatorship of capital over the state and over the popular vote, not only in Europe and America but in Asia and Africa.

The world wept because within the exploiting group of New World masters, greed and jealousy became so fierce that they fought for trade and markets and materials and slaves all over the world until at last in 1914 the world flamed in war. The fantastic structure fell, leaving grotesque Profits and Poverty, Plenty and Starvation, Empire and Democracy, staring at each other across World Depression. And the rebuilding, whether it comes now or a century later, will and must go back to the basic principles of Reconstruction in the United States during 1867–1876—Land, Light and Leading for slaves black, brown, yellow and white, under a dictatorship of the proletariat. . . .

Chapter XVI. Back Toward Slavery

The political success of the doctrine of racial separation, which overthrew Reconstruction by uniting the planter and the poor white, was far exceeded by its astonishing economic results. The theory of laboring class unity rests upon the assumption that laborers, despite internal jealousies, will unite because of their opposition to exploitation by the capitalists. According to this, even after a part of the poor white laboring class became identified with the planters, and eventually displaced them, their interests would be diametrically opposed to those of the mass of white labor, and of course to those of the black laborers. This would throw white and black labor into one class, and precipitate a united fight for higher wage and better working conditions.

Most persons do not realize how far this failed to work in the South, and it failed to work because the theory of race was supplemented by a carefully planned and slowly evolved method, which drove such a wedge between the white and black workers that there probably are not today in the world two groups of workers with practically identical interests who hate and fear each other so deeply and persistently and who are kept so far apart that neither sees anything of common interest.

It must be remembered that the white group of laborers, while they received a low wage, were compensated in part by a sort of public and psychological wage. They were given public deference and tides of courtesy because they were white. They were admitted freely with all classes of white people to public functions, public parks, and the best schools. The police were drawn from their ranks, and the courts, dependent upon their votes, treated them with such leniency as to encourage lawlessness. . . . On the other hand, in the same way, the Negro was subject to public insult; was afraid of mobs. . . . He was a caged human being. . . .

Some day it may burst in fire and blood. Who will be to blame? And where the greater cost? Black folk, after all, have little to lose, but Civilization has all.

This the American black man knows: his fight here is a fight to the finish. Either he dies or wins. If he wins it will be by no subterfuge or evasion of amalgamation. He will enter modern civilization here in America as a black man on terms of perfect and unlimited equality with any white man, or he will enter not at all. Either extermination root and branch, or absolute equality. There can be no compromise. This is the last great battle of the West. . . .

The unending tragedy of Reconstruction is the utter inability of the American mind to grasp its real significance, its national and worldwide implications. It was vain for Sumner and Stevens to hammer in the ears of the people that this problem involved the very foundations of American democracy, both political and economic. We are still too blind and infatuated to conceive of the emancipation of the laboring class in half the nation as a revolution comparable to the upheavals in France in the past, and in Russia, Spain, India and China today. . . . If the Reconstruction of the Southern states, from slavery to free labor, and from aristocracy to industrial democracy, had been conceived as a major national program of America, whose accomplishment at any price was well worth the effort, we should be living today in a different world.

The attempt to make black men American citizens was in a certain sense all a failure, but a splendid failure. It did not fail where it was expected to fail. It was *Athanasius contra mundum*, with back to the wall, outnumbered ten to one, with all the wealth and all the opportunity, and all the world against him. And only in his hands and heart the consciousness of a great and just cause; fighting the battle of all the oppressed and despised humanity of every race and color, against the massed hirelings of Religion, Science, Education, Law, and brute force.

8 | PHILADELPHIA: CRUCIBLE OF ABOLITION

Study Questions:

1. Why has Philadelphia played an outsized role in both state repression and abolitionist resistance?
2. What has abolition *meant* throughout Philadelphia's history, from the nineteenth century to today?

Key Organizations:

- Pennsylvania Abolitionist Society
- Free African Society
- Vigilance Committees
- Revolutionary Action Movement (RAM)
- MOVE Organization

Timeline:

- 1682—William Penn "purchases" territory from the Southern Unami Lenni Lenape.
- 1731—Benjamin Lay, dwarf, vegetarian, and radical abolitionist orator known as the "Quaker Comet," moves to Philadelphia.
- 1775—Pennsylvania Abolitionist Society is founded.
- 1787—Free African Society is founded.
- 1796—A Black woman is arrested for setting her master's house on fire.

- 1838—Abolitionist meeting in Pennsylvania Hall is attacked and the building is burned.
- 1842—Lombard Street Riots attack celebration of the abolition of slavery in the West Indies.
- 1931—Mass strike by hosiery workers has the city "on the brink of revolution."
- 1962—Revolutionary Action Movement (RAM) is founded in Philadelphia.
- 1972—Russell Maroon Shoatz is incarcerated.
- 1978—First MOVE standoff in Powelton.
- 1981—Mumia Abu-Jamal is arrested.
- 1985—Second MOVE standoff and bombing on Osage Avenue.

Mumia Abu-Jamal, *We Want Freedom* (2016 [2004])

Chapter 3, "A Panther Walks in Philly"

> "There is not perhaps anywhere to be found a city in which prejudice against color is more rampant than in Philadelphia. Hence all the incidents of caste are to be seen there in perfection. It has its white schools and its colored schools, its white churches and its colored churches, its white Christianity and its colored Christianity, its white concerts and its colored concerts, its white literary institutions and its colored institutions. —Frederick Douglass (ca. 1862)

When Frederick Douglass made this comment, he had spent over two decades living in freedom. He was personally familiar with Rochester, New York, the coastal regions of Maryland, Boston, and England, where he secured the funds to legally purchase his freedom. As an editor, writer, and abolitionist speaker of some renown, he undoubtedly traveled further than many, perhaps most men, white or Black, of his time. Here was a man who was a deep thinker, a sharp speaker, and an astute observer of life, with a broad range of experience. One wonders, why would Philadelphia bring so foul a taste to his distinguished palette?

In Philadelphia one finds the perfect example of American ambivalence on race. It is formally a northern city, but as it virtually straddles the mythical Mason-Dixon line, it is, in many ways, a southern city as well. It boasts the historical distinction of being the nation's first capital, the site of the signing of both the Declaration of Independence and the Constitution, but also of sustained racial and ethnic rivalry, conflict, and repression.

Known worldwide as an almost mythical birthplace of liberty, the hope of freedom acted as a kind of psychic magnet, drawing the poor and oppressed from the class-bound aristocracies of Europe in rivers of emigration, as well as Black captives escaping from southern bondage and Black freedmen and -women fleeing a humiliating and soul-sapping southern apartheid. The Philadelphia that the stalwart Frederick Douglass beheld with snarled contempt would more than double in size in half a century, rising from 650,000 people in 1860 to 1.5 million by 1914.

It was a city of extremes, with pronounced differences in wealth, power, and influence. For although millions of Europeans came to the English colonies with visions of a land where streets were paved with gold, they found cities awash in staggering poverty, with wealth concentrated in the hands of a few. The cities of the colonial era had almshouses or poorhouses, but these were hardly sufficient. "It is remarkable," one citizen of Philadelphia said in 1748, "what an increase of the number of beggars there is about this town this winter."

A century later, although the white working class could find work in cities, their standard of living was miserable. In Philadelphia, they lived fifty-five to a tenement, one room per family. There were no toilets and no garbage collection, and fresh water or even fresh air was virtually nonexistent. Many whites fought against their Black contemporaries' efforts to find work and tried to ensure they would not. Edward Abdy, a British visitor to Philadelphia in 1833, described the efforts of local Irish to remove Blacks from gainful employment. "Irish laborers were actively employed in this vile conspiracy against a people of whom they were jealous, "because they were more industrious, orderly and obliging than themselves." While Abdy's report may be influenced by the longstanding and deep-rooted antipathy between the British and the Irish, his remarks present evidence of what seemed to be deep anti-Black feeling among the Irish both in Philadelphia and New York:

> Forty years ago a colored man appeared, for the first time, as a carman in Philadelphia. Great jealousy was excited among that class of men; and every expedient was tried to get rid of a competitor whose success would draw others into the business. Threats and insults were followed by a report that he had been detected in stealing. The Quakers came forward to support him. They inquired into the grounds of the charge, and published its refutation. Their patronage maintained him in his situation, and encouraged others to follow his example. There are now plenty of them employed. At New York, a license cannot be obtained for them, and a black carman in that city is as rare as a black swan.

George Lippard is now forgotten, but before the work of Harriet Beecher Stowe stole the scene, he was the best-selling novelist in America. His 1844 novel *The Quaker City* told of a Philadelphia that was hideously violent, racist, and proud in its ignorance. He drew characters from the streets and headlines of the penny press, and one of his most memorable was an Irish rioter called Pump-Handle, who, in Irish-accented English, explained how he got his name:

> Why you see, a party of us one Sunday afternoon, had nothin' to do, so we got up a nigger riot. We have them things in Phil'delphy. Once or twice a year, you know? I helped to burn a nigger church, two orphans asylums and a school-house. And happenin' to have a handle in my hand, I aksedentally hit an old nigger on the head. Konsekance was he died. That's why they call me Pump-Handle.

Lippard, although a novelist, used his skills as a radical journalist to draw accurate portrayals of the city where he lived and worked.

What were not fictional, but strictly factual, were the scores of racist riots against Black achievement, abolitionism, and Black freedmen and women who lived in the city. Seven major mob attacks occurred between 1834 and 1838; among the most reported was the "Flying Horse Riot" of 1834. Radical and race historian Noel Ignatiev has written in his *How the Irish Became White*:

> On a lot near Seventh and South Streets in Philadelphia, an entrepreneur had for some time been operating a merry-go-round called, "Flying Horses." It was popular among both black people and whites, and served both "indiscriminately." Quarrels (not necessarily racial) over seating preference and so forth were frequent. On Tuesday evening, August 12, a mob of several hundred young White men, thought to be principally from outside the area, appeared at the scene, began fighting with the black people there, and in a very short time tore the merry-go-round to pieces. The mob then marched down South Street, to the adjacent township of Moyamensing, attacked a home occupied by a black family, and continued its violence

> on the small side streets where the black people mainly lived. On Wednesday evening a crowd wrecked the African Presbyterian Church on Seventh Street and a place several blocks away called the "Diving Bell," operated by "a white man, and used as a grog shop and lodging house for all colors, at the rate of three cents a head." After reducing these targets to ruins, the rioters began smashing windows, breaking down doors, and destroying furniture in private homes of Negroes, driving the inmates naked into the streets and beating any they caught. One correspondent reported that the mob threw a corpse out of a coffin, and cast a dead infant on the floor, "barbarously" mistreating its mother. "Some arrangement, it appears, existed between the mob and the white inhabitants, as the dwelling houses of the latter, contiguous to the residences of blacks, were illuminated, "and left undisturbed, while the huts of the negroes were signaled out with unerring certainty."

By midweek, when the fury had ebbed, several Blacks had been killed and two churches and at least twenty homes were destroyed. Hundreds of Blacks fled that part of town for other neighborhoods or sought refuge across the Delaware in New Jersey. This brutal violence, perpetrated by Irish gangs (many of them organized into the neighborhood fire companies), usually went unpunished. On the off chance that someone was arrested, Philadelphia juries duly acquitted them, especially when the victims were Black. The bloody and bitter feuds between the largely immigrant Catholics and the so-called nativists (other non-Catholic whites) often retreated when the target of local ire was a Black person or institution (such as a church). Then the nativist-Catholic divide would dissipate into whiteness against Blackness.

Three years after the terrorist violence of the Flying Horse Riot and the destruction of the Diving Bell, Pennsylvania Hall (built with Black and abolitionist money in Center City, Philadelphia) was burned to the ground by several thousand whites who disapproved of Blacks and whites coming together to meet and discuss the heated issue of the day—slavery. The nativist commander of the Philadelphia militia, Col. August James Pleasonton, who witnessed Pennsylvania Hall being consumed by the flames, would later note:

> There are serious apprehensions that the injudicious, to say the least, but as many think highly exciting and inflammatory proceedings of abolitionists, which have recently taken place here, and the disgusting intercourse between the whites and the blacks, as repugnant to all the prejudices of our education, which they not only have recommended, but are in the habit of practicing in this very Abolition Hall, will result in some terrible outbreak of popular indignation, not only against the Abolitionists, but also, against the colored people.

Pleasonton's view, aside from its elegant phrasing, could hardly be distinguished from that of the most uncouth Fenian of the period.

As for the cops or firemen of the day, little help could be expected from that quarter. Both, to the extent they existed at all, were little more than the accretion of local, ethnic street gangs who used their positions to scam and threaten people for money. These street gangs, for whom the fire company or the police were but an instrument, had names like the Rats, the Bleeders, the Blood Tubs, the Deathfetchers, and the Hyenas. It was for good reason that the American wit Mark Twain once quipped that people insured their homes, not against fire, but against the firemen. Failure to pay them might result in arson, a riot, or both!

This was the Philadelphia that Douglass loathed and perhaps feared.

It would be unfair and inaccurate to suggest that the anti-Black feeling in Philadelphia, or in other northern cities, for that matter, was the exclusive province of the white lower or working classes. At the highest levels of state and federal government, as well as in circles of wealth and influence, there was ample evidence of a pronounced antipathy for Blacks and of the fact that the popular rhetoric about "Philadelphia liberty" did not extend to them.

In 1837, a Pennsylvania constitutional convention overtly prevented Blacks from voting in the state.

At the time of the sensational Christiana Resistance in nearby Lancaster County, Pennsylvania, the *Philadelphia Bulletin* published an editorial that left no question as to whose side it defended in the conflict:

> Who is to prevail, the many or the few? The Old Saxon blood, which at vast sacrifice, founded these republics; or these African fugitives, whom we Pennsylvanians neither wish, nor will have? . . . Where the interests of two races come into collision, the weaker must yield, not merely as a matter of might, but, according to our republican doctrines of right also. Among ourselves, we whites understand this, and act upon this. . . .

Nor did the official voice of the state of Pennsylvania differ, in essence, from that of the bigotry of the *Bulletin* on the issue of liberty for those "African fugitives," in flight from bondage, who made their way to the "free" state. Margaret Morgan escaped from the slave system and fled to Pennsylvania in search of liberty. She found instead a state that spoke about freedom, but not for those who would seem to have needed it most—the enslaved.

When her capture by a Maryland slave-catcher was held to violate Pennsylvania's "personal liberty" laws, Maryland's attorney general argued, that the Constitution did not apply to Blacks. For they, as slaves, he argued, were not a party to the national pact and thus were not contained under the Preamble "We, the People." Pennsylvania agreed with her sister state, admitting their adversary's claims. Lawyers for Pennsylvania took what one legal scholar called a feeble position:

> Pennsylvania says: Instead of preventing you from taking your slaves, *we are anxious that you should have them; they are a population we do not covet*; and all our legislation tends toward giving you every facility to get them; but we do claim the right of legislating upon this subject so as to bring you under legal restraint, which will prevent you from taking a freeman.

As might be expected of a court composed predominantly of slave owners, the Supreme Court held for Edward Prigg, agent of the slave owner, and overturned Pennsylvania's "personal liberty" law as unconstitutional. For Margaret Morgan and her children—including her youngest, born into a "free" state—the Court's majority opinion meant a return to bondage.

The majority opinion in *Prigg v. Pennsylvania* (1842), penned by Justice Joseph Story of Massachusetts, made it clear that the state's claim to "personal liberty" applied to everyone, except slaves:

> The rights of the owners of fugitive slaves are in no just sense interfered with, or regulated by such a course. . . . But such regulations can never be permitted to interfere with or to obstruct the just rights of the owner to reclaim his slave,

> derived from the Constitution of the United States; or with the remedies prescribed by Congress to aid and enforce the same.
>
> Upon these grounds, we are of opinion that the act of Pennsylvania upon which this indictment is founded, is unconstitutional and void. It purports to punish as a public offence against the state, the very act of seizing and removing a slave by his master, which the Constitution of the United States was designed to justify and uphold.

The *Prigg* case would prove a harbinger of the judicial insults to come, among them, *Dred Scott v. Sanford,* decided nearly a decade later. The *Prigg* case was also a precursor of the infamous Fugitive Slave Law of 1850. Pennsylvania's lawyers betrayed Margaret Morgan, her five children, and thousands like her throughout the northern state. Instead of defending liberty, they defended comity between sister states and, by extension, the legality of slavery. Once again, the courts favored the illusion of human beings as property, as chattel, rather than the reality of humans yearning for liberty from base tyranny.

Philadelphia Modernity

The Philadelphia of the mid-twentieth century remained a conflicted, class-conscious, racially stratified city.

Black Philadelphia's population burgeoned, fueled in large part by the Great Migration which sent wave upon wave of a Black rural flood into urban centers like Pittsburgh, New York, Chicago, Boston, San Francisco, Seattle, and Oakland. In these centers were established de facto Black Quarters, areas of containment and isolation, policed by law and social custom to minimize and restrict Black movement, mobility, and dispersal.

Ghettos are not natural growths, like bunions; they are legal constructs that are the fruit of the long-held beliefs and practices of segregation, and they survived its alleged death through restrictive covenants that forbade the selling of millions of units of housing to African Americans. This legal restriction had its equally effective corollary in social and customary practices of pricing property at rates that were prohibitive to the vast majority of the ghetto population.

Over the generations, central North Philadelphia, West Philadelphia, Southwest Philadelphia, and, to a lesser extent, small pockets of South Philadelphia became shorthand for Black Philadelphia. This did not mean these were the only places one found Black inhabitants, but it meant these areas were ones where Blacks dwelt in predominance.

Conversely, there were areas of the city, notably Northeast Philadelphia, East Oak Lane, Kensington, and South Philadelphia, where Black folks walked, drove, or strove to live and work at their peril. To see Black homes marred by racist graffiti or firebombed by whites dwelling in neighboring homes was not an odd occurrence in the city with a name meaning Brotherly Love. Nor was it a rare occurrence for a Black pedestrian to be put to the chase for daring to walk in a "white" neighborhood.

These private, communal acts were echoed by official ones, done in the name of the city, by the police. Black Philadelphians came of age with the deeply felt knowledge that they could be beaten, wounded, or killed by cops with virtual impunity. The predominantly white police seemed like foreigners in a dark village who treated their alleged fellow citizens with the vehemence one reserves for an enemy. For ghetto youth, this took the form of the police using the maddened self-hatred and regional antipathy between youth of various gangs to foment yet more hatred and violent reprisal. One favorite tactic they routinely utilized was to pick up a few youngsters from one gang, place them in a patrol car, drive them to enemy gang turf, let them out of the vehicle, and scream curses and insults against the enemy gang. To the young men left standing as the cop car raced off at breakneck speed, their choices were few and unenviable: stand and fight against the swarm of sworn enemies or run like the devil, hoping to get to safe territory before they got badly beaten, shot, or worse.

It is into this milieu that the Black Panther Party came into being in Philadelphia. Once the chapter was formed, other questions remained. What would this new organization do? How would we let folks know we existed? What would be our focus? These were but some of the challenges facing the group and met by the late spring of 1969:

> With the renting, repair, cleaning, and painting of the storefront at 1928 West Columbia Avenue, the local party would have its first formal presence (odd apartments and private homes had sufficed previously), a reliable place where people could contact us. The time could not have been more perfect for our arrival, for the clear air, the bright sky blue, the very essence of the season of new life was upon us. As soon as we had finished painting the walls (Panther powder blue, with black glaze adorning the moldings), affixed a few posters to the walls (Malcolm X, Che Guevara, Huey and Bobby, armed), and used pressure-sensitive letters to inscribe the inside of the fronting glass with the black, capital, gold-edged letters, people began appearing at our door. What drew them was the bold letters blaring from the window: BLACK PANTHER PARTY.
>
> That seemingly simple message drew in the young, the old, and those in the middle, from the cautious to the curious. Students came in, eager to sell the paper.

Even the established, like the real estate owner who rented the property to the Party and who owned properties all around the neighborhood took pains to demonstrate his nationalist credentials. He confided to us that he went to the historically Black college, Lincoln University, with the revered Kwame Nkrumah, the first President of the independent West African nation of Ghana.

But to have an office was not enough. The fledgling organization had to do something. After much thought, and a request from the national office, the captain ordered us to assemble at the State Building, at Broad and Spring Garden Streets, near the center of the city, to demonstrate for the freedom of the imprisoned BPP Minister of Defense, Huey P. Newton, who was facing murder charges stemming from a car stop and shoot-out in Oakland. The objective was to snag some publicity for the Party, and thus to inform the city's huge Black population of our presence.

The date is May 1, 1969, and between fifteen and twenty of us are in the full uniform of black berets, black jackets of smooth leather, and black trousers. As we assemble, a rousing chant of "Free Huey!" is raised. Leaflets are distributed to passersby, and we are able to inform some people of our presence and how to contact us.

Several of Huey's articles are read over the megaphone, and, before long, we have a somewhat rousing rally on our hands. Some of the excited kids from the nearby Ben Franklin High School cut their classes to attend the rally, and several papers are sold. Captain Reggie reads from Huey's "In Defense of Self-Defense," which noted, in part:

> The heirs of Malcolm now stand millions strong on their corner of the triangle, facing the racist dog oppressor and the soulless endorsed spokesmen. The heirs of Malcolm have picked up the gun and taking first things first are moving to expose the endorsed spokesmen so the Black masses can see them for what they are and have always been. The choice offered by the heirs of Malcolm to the endorsed spokesmen is to repudiate the oppressor and crawl back to their own people and earn a speedy reprieve or face a merciless, speedy, and most timely execution for treason and being "too wrong for too long."

Cameras went off like popcorn, but we had no real idea who the mostly white photographers were. We assumed they were the press, but some had the unmistakable air of cops about them. It never dawned on us that some were FBI agents building a file on us. Mostly, it was because, in an age of global revolution, it didn't seem too extraordinary to be a revolutionary. Didn't America come into being by way of the American Revolution?

Here we were, reading the hard, uncompromising words of the Minister of Defense of the Black Panther Party at the State Building in the heart of the fourth largest city in America, while red-faced, nervous, armed cops stood around on the periphery of our rally . . . what did we think would happen? We thought, in the amorphous realm of hope, youth, and boundless optimism, that revolution was virtually a heartbeat away. It was four years since Malcolm's assassination and just over a year since the assassination of the Rev. Martin Luther King,

Jr. The Vietnam War was flaring up under Nixon's Vietnamization program, and the rising columns of smoke from Black rebellions in Watts, Detroit, Newark, and North Philly could still be sensed—their ashen smoldering still tasted in the air.

Huey was our leader, and we felt, with utter certainty, that he spoke for the vast majority of Black folks. He certainly spoke for us. We loved and revered him and wondered why everybody else didn't feel the same way. Our job was to make all see this obvious truth. His work moved us all deeply, and we believed we could in turn move the world. This feeling motivated us to sell The Black Panther newspaper with passion and spirit, for Huey himself had written that "a newspaper is the voice of the party, the voice of the Panther must be heard throughout the land."

We struggled daily to make it so. We got up early and didn't go to sleep until late. For most of us, Party work was all that we did, all day, into the night. Our little branch blossomed into the biggest, most productive chapter in the state and one of the most vigorous in the nation. A year after our rally, our branch sold 10,000 Party newspapers a week and had functioning Party offices in West Philadelphia and Germantown. The Party nationally sold nearly 150,000 papers through direct street sales and paid subscriptions per week. The Party was literally growing by leaps and bounds, both locally and nationally. From our original fifteen-odd members in the spring of 1969, a year later virtually ten times that number would call themselves members of the Black Panther Party of Philadelphia.

We spoke at antiwar rallies. We attended school meetings. We met with high school students. We met in churches. We worked with gangs and provided transportation to area prisons. Everywhere we went, we brought along the Ten-Point Program and Platform of the Black Panther Party, as a guideline for our organizing efforts. By any measure, we made an impressive beginning.

It was May 1969.

A young man named O.J. Simpson had just been named the number one NFL draft pick by Buffalo, a year after winning the Heisman for his performance as running back for University of Southern California. The album Blood, Sweat and Tears (by the group Blood, Sweat and Tears) would win the best album Grammy. The Oscar for Best Picture would be awarded to Midnight Cowboy. The great Muhammad Ali had been stripped of his heavyweight boxing crown two years previous, and the championship was vacant. The number one first-round draft pick for the NBA was a lanky, Afro-coifed youth named Lew Alcindor of UCLA, who went to Milwaukee.

In April, the US military had mobilized its biggest troop deployment of 543,400 soldiers. In just three months, half a million young folks would gather in a remote corner of New York called Woodstock. Shortly thereafter, a quarter million people would march in front of the White House demanding an end to the Vietnam War. Before the month of May ended, a police raid in New Haven, Connecticut, would threaten the very stability of the Party. Chairman Bobby Seale and Ericka Huggins would face murder charges. In all, eight Panthers would be arrested, and at least one would agree to turn state's evidence. If convicted, Seale would face the electric chair.

9 | DECOLONIZATION & THIRD WORLD REVOLUTION

Study Questions:

1. Why is decolonization "always a violent event" for Fanon?
2. What does decolonization mean for Palestine today? For the United States?
3. Who is decolonization *for*?

Key Concepts:

- Colonialism: domination of a territory through small-scale outposts or large-scale settler colonialism for the purpose of extracting land, labor, markets, and resources.
- Imperialism: foreign political and economic domination of resources and global markets, and the inter-imperial competition and conflict this unleashes.
- Decolonization: narrowly, the process of liberating colonies from European domination, especially in early nineteenth-century Latin America and mid twentieth-century Africa and Asia.

Claude McKay, "If We Must Die" (1919)

If we must die, let it not be like hogs
Hunted and penned in an inglorious spot,

While round us bark the mad and hungry dogs,
Making their mock at our accursèd lot.
If we must die, O let us nobly die,
So that our precious blood may not be shed
In vain; then even the monsters we defy
Shall be constrained to honor us though dead!
O kinsmen! we must meet the common foe!
Though far outnumbered let us show us brave,
And for their thousand blows deal one death-blow!
What though before us lies the open grave?
Like men we'll face the murderous, cowardly pack,
Pressed to the wall, dying, but fighting back!

Refaat Alareer, "If I Must Die" (2023)

If I must die,
you must live
to tell my story
to sell my things
to buy a piece of cloth
and some strings,
(make it white with a long tail)
so that a child, somewhere in Gaza
while looking heaven in the eye
awaiting his dad who left in a blaze—
and bid no one farewell
not even to his flesh
not even to himself—
sees the kite, my kite you made, flying up above
and thinks for a moment an angel is there
bringing back love

If I must die
let it bring hope
let it be a tale

Frantz Fanon, *The Wretched of the Earth* (1961)

On Violence

National liberation, national reawakening, restoration of the nation to the people or Commonwealth, whatever the name used, whatever the latest expression, decolonization is always a violent event. At whatever level we study it—individual encounters, a change of name for a sports club, the guest list at a cocktail party, members of a police force or the board of directors of a state or private bank—decolonization is quite simply the substitution of one "species" of mankind by another. The substitution is unconditional, absolute, total, and seamless. We could go on to portray the rise of a new nation, the establishment of a new state, its diplomatic relations and its economic and political orientation. But instead we have decided to describe the kind of tabula rasa which from the outset defines any decolonization. What is singularly important is that it starts from the very first day with the basic claims of the colonized. In actual fact, proof of success lies in a social fabric that has been changed inside out. This change is extraordinarily important because it is desired, clamored for, and demanded. The need for this change exists in a raw, repressed, and reckless state in the lives and consciousness of colonized men and women. But the eventuality of such a change is also experienced as a terrifying future in the consciousness of another "species" of men and women: the *colons*, the colonists.

***

Decolonization, which sets out to change the order of the world, is clearly an agenda for total disorder. But it cannot be accomplished by the wave of a magic wand, a natural cataclysm, or a gentleman's agreement. Decolonization, we know, is an historical process: In other words, it can only be understood, it can only find its significance and become self coherent insofar as we can discern the history-making movement which gives it form and substance. Decolonization is the encounter between two congenitally antagonistic forces that in fact owe their singularity to the kind of reification secreted and nurtured by the colonial situation. Their first confrontation was colored by violence and their cohabitation—or rather the exploitation of the colonized by the colonizer—continued at the point of the bayonet and under cannon fire. The colonist and the colonized are old acquaintances. And consequently, the colonist is right when he says he "knows" them. It is the colonist who *fabricated* and *continues to fabricate* the colonized subject. The colonist derives his validity, i.e., his wealth, from the colonial system.

Decolonization never goes unnoticed, for it focuses on and fundamentally alters being, and transforms the spectator crushed to a nonessential state into a privileged actor, captured in a virtually grandiose fashion by the spotlight of History. It infuses a new rhythm, specific to a new generation of men, with a new language and a new humanity. Decolonization is truly the creation of new men. But such a creation cannot be attributed to a supernatural power: The "thing" colonized becomes a man through the very process of liberation. Decolonization, therefore, implies the urgent need to thoroughly challenge the colonial situation. Its definition can, if we want to describe it accurately, be summed up in the well-known words: "The last shall be first." Decolonization is verification of this. At a descriptive level, therefore, any decolonization is a success.

***

In its bare reality, decolonization reeks of red-hot cannonballs and bloody knives. For the last can be the first only after a murderous and decisive confrontation between the two protagonists. This determination to have the last move up to the front, to have them clamber up (too quickly, say some) the famous echelons of an organized society, can only succeed by resorting to every means, including, of course, violence.

You do not disorganize a society, however primitive it may be, with such an agenda if you are not determined from the very start to smash every obstacle encountered. The colonized, who have made up their mind to make such an agenda into a driving force, have been prepared for violence from time immemorial. As soon as they are born it is obvious to them that their cramped world, riddled with taboos, can only be challenged by out and out violence.

The colonial world is a compartmentalized world. It is obviously as superfluous to recall the existence of "native" towns and European towns, of schools for "natives" and schools for Europeans, as it is to recall apartheid in South Africa. Yet if we penetrate inside this compartmentalization we shall at least bring to light some of its key aspects. By penetrating its geographical configuration and classification we shall be able to delineate the backbone on which the decolonized society is reorganized.

The colonized world is a world divided in two. The dividing line, the border, is represented by the barracks and the police stations. In the colonies, the official, legitimate agent, the spokesperson for the colonizer and the regime of oppression, is the police officer or the soldier. In capitalist societies, education, whether secular or religious, the teaching of moral reflexes handed down from father to son, the exemplary integrity of workers decorated after fifty years of loyal and faithful service, the fostering of love for harmony and wisdom, those aesthetic forms of respect for the status quo, instill in the exploited a mood of submission and inhibition which considerably eases the task of the agents of law and order. In capitalist countries a multitude of sermonizers, counselors, and "confusion-mongers" intervene between the exploited and the authorities. In colonial regions, however, the proximity and frequent, direct intervention by the police and the military ensure the colonized are kept under close scrutiny, and contained by rifle butts and napalm. We have seen how the government's agent uses a language of pure violence. The agent does not alleviate oppression or mask domination. He displays and demonstrates them with the clear conscience of the law enforcer, and brings violence into the homes and minds of the colonized subject.

The "native" sector is not complementary to the European sector. The two confront each other, but not in the service of a higher unity. Governed by a purely Aristotelian logic, they follow the dictates of mutual exclusion: There is no conciliation possible, one of them is superfluous. The colonist's sector is a sector built to last, all stone and steel. It's a sector of lights and paved roads, where the trash cans constantly overflow with strange and wonderful garbage, undreamed-of leftovers. The colonist's feet can never be glimpsed, except perhaps in the sea, but then you can never get close enough. They are protected by solid shoes in a sector where the streets are clean and smooth, without a pothole, without a stone. The colonist's sector is a sated, sluggish sector, its belly is permanently full of good things. The colonist's sector is a white folks' sector, a sector of foreigners.

The colonized's sector, or at least the "native" quarters, the shanty town, the Medina, the reservation, is a disreputable place inhabited by disreputable people. You are born anywhere, anyhow. You die anywhere, from anything. It's a world with no space, people are piled one on top of the other, the shacks squeezed tightly together. The colonized's sector is a famished sector, hungry for bread, meat, shoes, coal, and light. The colonized's sector is a sector that crouches and cowers, a sector on its knees, a sector that is prostrate. It's a sector of niggers, a sector of towelheads. The gaze that the colonized subject casts at the colonist's sector is a look of lust, a look of envy. Dreams of possession. Every type of possession: of sitting at the colonist's table and sleeping in his bed, preferably with his wife. The colonized man is an envious man. The colonist is aware of this as he catches the furtive glance, and constantly on his guard, realizes bitterly that: "They want to take our place." And it's true there is not one colonized subject who at least once a day does not dream of taking the place of the colonist.

This compartmentalized world, this world divided in two, is inhabited by different species. The singularity of the colonial context lies in the fact that economic reality, inequality, and enormous disparities in lifestyles never manage to mask the human reality. Looking at the immediacies of the colonial context, it is clear that what divides this world is first and foremost what species, what race one belongs to. In the colonies the economic infrastructure is also a superstructure. The cause is effect: You are rich because you are white, you are white because you are rich. This is why a Marxist analysis should always be slightly stretched when it comes to addressing the colonial issue. It is not just the concept of the precapitalist society, so effectively studied by Marx, which needs to be reexamined here. The serf is essentially different from the knight, but a reference to divine right is needed to justify this difference in status. In the colonies the foreigner imposed himself using his cannons and machines. Despite the success of his pacification, in spite of his appropriation, the colonist always remains a foreigner. It is not the factories, the estates, or the bank account which primarily characterize the "ruling class." The ruling species is first and foremost the outsider from elsewhere, different from the indigenous population, "the others."

The violence which governed the ordering of the colonial world, which tirelessly punctuated the destruction of the indigenous social fabric, and demolished unchecked the systems of reference of the country's economy, lifestyles, and modes of dress, this same violence will be vindicated and appropriated when, taking history into their own hands, the colonized swarm into the forbidden cities. To blow the colonial world to smithereens is henceforth a clear image within the grasp and imagination of every colonized subject. To dislocate the colonial world does not mean that once the borders have been eliminated there will be a right of way between the two sectors. To destroy the colonial world means nothing less than demolishing the colonist's sector, burying it deep within the earth or banishing it from the territory.

Challenging the colonial world is not a rational confrontation of viewpoints. It is not a discourse on the universal, but the impassioned claim by the colonized that their world is fundamentally different. The colonial world is a Manichaean world . . . Sometimes this Manichaeanism reaches its logical conclusion and dehumanizes the colonized subject. In plain talk, he is reduced to the state of an animal. And consequently, when the colonist speaks of the colonized he uses zoological terms. . . . The colonized know all that and roar with laughter every time they hear themselves called an animal by the other. For they know they are not animals. And at the very moment when they discover their humanity, they begin to sharpen their weapons to secure its victory.

EZLN, "First Declaration of the Lacandón Jungle" (1994)

Today We Say: Enough is Enough!

To the People of Mexico:
Mexican Brothers and Sisters:

We are a product of 500 years of struggle: first against slavery, then during the War of Independence against Spain led by insurgents, then to avoid being absorbed by North American imperialism, then to promulgate our constitution and expel the French empire from our soil, and later the dictatorship of Porfirio Diaz denied us the just application of the Reform laws and the people rebelled and leaders like Villa and Zapata emerged, poor men just like us. We have been denied the most elemental preparation so they can use us as cannon fodder and pillage the wealth of our country. They don't care that we have nothing, absolutely nothing, not even a roof over our heads, no land, no work, no health care, no food nor education. Nor are we able to freely and democratically elect our political representatives, nor is there independence from foreigners, nor is there peace nor justice for ourselves and our children.

But today, we say ENOUGH IS ENOUGH. We are the inheritors of the true builders of our nation. The dispossessed, we are millions and we thereby call upon our brothers and sisters to join this struggle as the only path, so that we will not die of hunger due to the insatiable ambition of a 70 year dictatorship led by a clique of traitors that represent the most conservative and sell-out groups. They are the same ones that opposed Hidalgo and Morelos, the same ones that betrayed Vicente Guerrero, the same ones that sold half our country to the foreign invader, the same ones that imported a European prince to rule our country, the same ones that formed the "scientific" Porfirista dictatorship, the same ones that opposed the Petroleum Expropriation, the same ones that massacred the railroad workers in 1958 and the students in 1968, the same ones that today take everything from us, absolutely everything.

To prevent the continuation of the above and as our last hope, after having tried to utilize all legal means based on our Constitution, we go to our Constitution, to apply Article 39 which says: "National Sovereignty essentially and originally resides in the people. All political power emanates from the people and its purpose is to help the people. The people have, at all times, the inalienable right to alter or modify their form of government." Therefore, according to our constitution, we declare the following to the Mexican federal army, the pillar of the Mexican dictatorship that we suffer from, monopolized by a one-party system and led by Carlos Salinas de Gortari, the maximum and illegitimate federal executive that today holds power.

According to this Declaration of War, we ask that other powers of the nation advocate to restore the legitimacy and the stability of the nation by overthrowing the dictator.

We also ask that international organizations and the International Red Cross watch over and regulate our battles, so that our efforts are carried out while still protecting our civilian population. We declare now and always that we are subject to the Geneva Accord, forming the EZLN as our fighting arm of our liberation struggle. We have the Mexican people on our side, we have the beloved tri-colored flag highly respected by our insurgent fighters. We use black and red in our uniform as our symbol of our working people on strike. Our flag carries the following letters, "EZLN," Zapatista Army of National Liberation, and we always carry our flag into combat.

Beforehand, we refuse any effort to disgrace our just cause by accusing us of being drug traffickers, drug guerrillas, thieves, or other names that might by used by our enemies. Our struggle follows the constitution which is held high by its call for justice and equality.

Therefore, according to this declaration of war, we give our military forces, the EZLN, the following orders:

- First: Advance to the capital of the country, overcoming the Mexican federal army, protecting in our advance the civilian population and permitting the people in the liberated area the right to freely and democratically elect their own administrative authorities.
- Second: Respect the lives of our prisoners and turn over all wounded to the International Red Cross.
- Third: Initiate summary judgements against all soldiers of the Mexican federal army and the political police that have received training or have been paid by foreigners, accused of being traitors to our country, and against all those that have repressed and treated badly the civil population and robbed or stolen from or attempted crimes against the good of the people.
- Fourth: Form new troops with all those Mexicans that show their interest in joining our struggle, including those that, being enemy soldiers, turn themselves in without having fought against us, and promise to take orders from the General Command of the Zapatista Army of National Liberation.
- Fifth: We ask for the unconditional surrender of the enemy's headquarters before we begin any combat to avoid any loss of lives.
- Sixth: Suspend the robbery of our natural resources in the areas controlled by the EZLN.

To the People of Mexico: We, the men and women, full and free, are conscious that the war that we have declared is our last resort, but also a just one. The dictators have been applying an undeclared genocidal war against our people for many years. Therefore we ask for your participation, your decision to support this plan that struggles for work, land, housing, food, health care, education, independence, freedom, democracy, justice and peace. We declare that we will not stop fighting until the basic demands of our people have been met by forming a government of our country that is free and democratic.

The Red Nation, *The Red Deal* (2021)

The crux of the so-called "Indian problem" in the Western Hemisphere hinges on this question: "What do Indians want?" For us, it's a larger social problem of underdevelopment. Colonialism has deprived Indigenous people, and all people who are affected by it, of the means to develop according to our needs, principles, and values. It begins with the land. We have been made "Indians" only because we have the most precious commodity to the settler states: land. Vigilante, cop, and soldier often stand between us, our connections to the land, and justice. "Land back" strikes fear in the heart of the settler. But as we show here, it's the soundest environmental policy for a planet teetering on the brink of total ecological collapse. The path forward is simple: it's decolonization or extinction. And that starts with land back.

In 2019, the mainstream environmental movement—largely dominated by middle- and upper-class liberals of the Global North—adopted as its symbolic leader a teenage Swedish girl who crossed the Atlantic in a boat to the Americas. But we have our own heroes. Water protectors at Standing Rock ushered in a new era of militant land defense. They are the bellwethers of our generation. The Year of the Water Protector, 2016, was also the hottest year on record and sparked a different kind of climate justice movement. Alexandria Ocasio-Cortez, herself a water protector, began her successful bid for Congress while in the prayer camps at Standing Rock. With Senator Ed Markey, she proposed a Green New Deal in 2019. Standing Rock, however, was part of a constellation of Indigenous-led uprisings across North America and the US-occupied Pacific: Dooda Desert Rock (2006), Unist'ot'en Camp (2010), Keystone XL (2011), Idle No More (2012), Trans Mountain (2013), Enbridge Line 3 (2014), Protect Mauna Kea (2014), Save Oak Flat (2015), Nihígaal Bee Iiná (2015), Bayou Bridge (2017), O'odham Anti-Border Collective (2019), Kumeyaay Defense Against the Wall (2020), and 1492 Land Back Lane (2020), among many more.

Each movement rises against colonial and corporate extractive projects. But what's often downplayed is the revolutionary potency of what Indigenous resistance stands for: caretaking and creating just relations between human and other-than-human worlds on a planet thoroughly devastated by capitalism. The image of the water protector and the slogan "Water is Life!" are catalysts of this generation's climate justice movement. Both are political positions grounded in decolonization—a project that isn't exclusively about the Indigenous. Anyone who walked through the gates of prayer camps at Standing Rock, regardless of whether they were Indigenous or not, became a water protector. Each carried the embers of that revolutionary potential back to their home communities. Water protectors were on the frontlines of distributing mutual aid to communities in need throughout the pandemic. Water protectors were in the streets of Seattle, Portland, Minneapolis, Albuquerque, and many other cities in the summer of 2020 as police stations burned and monuments to genocide collapsed. The state responds to water protectors—those who care for and defend life—with an endless barrage of batons, felonies, shackles, and chemical weapons. If they weren't before, our eyes are now open: the police and the military, driven by settler and imperialist rage, are holding back the climate justice movement.

Decolonization

In this era of catastrophic climate change, why is it easier for some to imagine the end of fossil fuels than settler colonialism? To imagine green economies, carbon-free wind and solar energy, and electric, bullet-train utopias but not the return of Indigenous lands? Why is it easier to imagine the end of the world—a zombie apocalypse—than the end of capitalism? It's not an either/or scenario. Ending settler colonialism and capitalism and returning Indigenous lands are all possible—and necessary.

The question of restoring Indigenous land to Indigenous people is thoroughly political, which means the theft of it was—and is—not inevitable or beyond our current capacities to resolve. The same goes for Black reparations, ending the hardening of the US border, defunding US imperialism, and stopping the continued exploitation of resources and labor in the Global South by countries up north. "The issue is that accumulation-based societies don't like the answers we come up with because they are not quick technological fixes, they are not easy," Michi Saagiig Nichnaabeg scholar Leanne Betasamosake Simpson has said.

Fifty years ago, decolonization—nations freeing themselves from colonial rule—and land reform inspired global visions for a socialist future, advancing the class struggle further than it has ever gone before by raising the living standards of billions in the Global South. Some Western socialists seem to have abandoned that future in favor of technological pipe dreams like mining asteroids, gene editing, and synthetic meat, without addressing the real problem of overconsumption in the Global North, which is directly enabled by the dispossession of Indigenous and Black life and imperial wars in the Global South. We need a revolution of values that recenters relationships to one another and the Earth over profits.

Anti-Imperialism

The geopolitical relationship countries like the United States have with the rest of the world is deeply intertwined with settler colonialism. Imperial projects build upon settler colonial ones. For the last twenty years, we've seen the United States destroy countries and communities in a quest for oil. The invasion of Iraq in 2003 was for oil. Cultural treasures from one of the oldest civilizations on the planet were destroyed in the first days of the invasion, but the US military and its mercenary contractors chose to guard oil infrastructure. . . . In 2002, Bush sponsored a coup d'état against Venezuela's democratically elected president Hugo Chávez, who came to power on a promise to nationalize the corrupt oil sector to fund national infrastructure and poverty relief programs for the poor. When Obama assumed office in January 2009, he continued Bush's sanctions against Venezuela and other nations deemed hostile to US interests. . . .

Increasingly, there is a direct link to the ongoing Venezuelan crisis and oil production in North America. When global oil prices began to fall due to the North American oil boom, a crisis ensued in Venezuela, and the money used to fund the social progress of the country's poorest was all but halted. . . . In other words, because of US intervention, economies of the Global South are not allowed to develop to a point where they can transition away from fossil fuels. Therefore, any climate policy must also be anti-imperialist, demanding an immediate end to genocidal sanctions and the payment of northern climate debt to the rest of the world. . . .

Prison abolition and an end to border imperialism are key aspects of the Red Deal, for good reason. The GND calls for the creation of millions of "green" jobs, as well as a policy of "just transition" for poor and working-class families and communities that currently depend on resource extraction for basic income and needs, and which will suffer greatly when the extractive industry is shut down. In the United States today, however, about seventy million people—nearly one-third of adults—have some kind of criminal conviction—whether or not they've served time—that prevents them from holding certain kinds of jobs. If we add this number of people to the approximately eight million undocumented migrants, the sum is about half the US workforce, two-thirds of whom are not white. *Half* of the workforce faces employment discrimination because of mass criminalization and incarceration.

The terrorization of Black, Indigenous, Brown, migrant, and poor communities by border enforcement agencies and the police drives down wages and disciplines poor people—whether or not they are working—by keeping them in a state of perpetual uncertainty and precarity. As extreme weather and imperialist interventions continue to fuel migration, especially from Central America, the policies of punishment—such as walls, detention camps, and increased border security—continue to feed capital with cheap, throwaway lives. The question of citizenship—colonizing settler nations have no right to say who does and doesn't belong—is something that will have to be thoroughly challenged as a "legal" privilege to life chances. Equitable access to employment and social care must break down imperial borders, not reproduce them. . . .

A Caretaking Economy

A new green economy is the antithesis of what currently exists: a militarized extractive economy, what Lakotas call *"owasicu owe,"* the fat-taker, the colonizer, the capitalist economy; or what activist Winona LaDuke calls "*Weitiko*"—the cannibal economy. If prisons, police, and the military are the caretakers of violence and agents of death, then educators, healthcare workers, counselors, water protectors, and land defenders are caretakers of peace and agents of life. A green economy should be born from, and center the labor and needs of, caretakers. Indigenous people, for example, are already working "green jobs," they're just not getting paid or enjoying the protections employment offers for land, water, and treaty defense. Caretaking is often unrecognized work that is heavily gendered, severely criminalized, and never fairly compensated. The pay gaps between carceral and military workers (mostly men), and care workers (mostly women), makes this crystal clear. The climate justice movement needs to center the labor struggle of caretakers if it is to be successful. Caretakers can be powerful authors of a new economic system to replace capitalism through a caretaking economy.

This caretaking economy is already in place. Three-quarters of land-based environments and two-thirds of marine environments have been affected by capitalist development, but environmental degradation has been less severe in places managed by Indigenous peoples and local communities. While making up only 5 percent of the world's population, Indigenous peoples protect 80 percent of the planet's biodiversity. Indigenous peoples and local communities who have distinct cultural and social ties to ancestral homelands and bioregions still caretake at least a quarter of the world's land. This includes places that are the lungs of the world, such as the Amazon rainforest, and its veins, like the Missouri River Basin—areas facing existential threats of deforestation, damming, water contamination, oil and gas development, and mining. Indigenous people protect the land, air, and water we all need to live. . . .

Land Back

The best forms of environmental policy come from the bottom up, and momentous change only happens with the might of a peoples' movement behind it. In North America, change begins with the land—one of the primary sources of both wealth and inequality. . . . Indigenous laws and governance systems would reemerge in place of federal Indian law. Treaties would be enforced, not by the US government, but by Indigenous nations. Land back would become mandatory, ushering in a different type of development and reconstruction of our fundamental relationship to land not premised on ownership but on collective well-being. Transforming our relationship with the land would create conditions for caretakers (who aren't exclusively Indigenous) to inherit the Earth; to work with, take care of, restore, and heal the land as diverse workers whose labor is bound, quite literally, with the land itself. We are citizens of a land that has yet to be brought into existence, but nonetheless exists in the recesses of our long historical memories and revolutionary imagination.

The focus, however, is not just on land within what is the "domestic" territory of the United States. Demilitarization also means land back to the nations and territories occupied by one of more than 800 overseas US military bases that violate sovereignty and deny self-determination to millions: Guantanamo Bay, Okinawa, Korea, Guam, Hawai'i, the Philippines, Iraq, Egypt, Afghanistan, Puerto Rico, El Salvador, Honduras, Panama, and so many other places the US occupies. Land back means the return of just relations between the human world and the other-than-human world. It means removing the overseas US military threat that encircles and bullies other nations. Land back is about justice and about bringing in a new world based on peace and cooperation, not coercion and force.

It's Not Just an "Indian Problem"

While Indigenous people are framed as the age-old "Indian problem," decolonization and land back aren't just an Indian problem. If every struggle were made into a climate struggle—which must be done if we are to have a future on this planet—then every struggle in North America must be made into a struggle for decolonization. The solutions offered in *The Red Deal* must entail a revolution that turns back the forces of destruction. It must penetrate the economic and cultural realms with equal urgency and force. Indigenous peoples should be empowered to develop and implement restorative practices according to their own customs and traditions. Caretakers should not hesitate to take the reins of leadership. The energies and passions of Indigenous peoples at the forefront of resisting extractive capitalism should inspire everyone, as water protectors and land defenders have inspired a generation of climate justice revolutionaries. Indigenous demands for the restoration of land, air, and water are essential for the return of our collective humanity. This is the vision and the mandate of the Red Deal: uniting Indigenous and non-Indigenous people in a common struggle to save the Earth.

Indigenous political structures and economic systems do not apply only to Indigenous people. Our liberation is bound to the liberation of all humans and the planet. What we seek is a world premised on Indigenous *values* of interspecies responsibility and balance. We seek to uplift knowledges, technologies, governance structures, and economic strategies that will make these values possible, in the immediate future and in the long term, and which always have the future health of the land at the center of their design and implementation, Indigenous or not. In this sense, decolonization is for, and benefits, everyone. It also needs our collective cooperation to succeed.

10 | WHAT IS THE STATE? WHAT IS REVOLUTION?

Study Questions:

1. What is "The State"? Where do we confront it on an everyday basis?
2. How do we resist the state? Engage with it? Leverage it? Avoid it?
3. Where is *our* power located, if not in the state?
4. Is the dictatorship of the proletariat a state? Why or why not?
5. Does abolition mean abolishing the state? If so, how?
6. Are all "states" the same?

Key Concepts:

- Dictatorship of the Proletariat: a temporary, transitional stage after the proletariat seizes power, using the weapons at its disposal to defeat its enemies, suppress capitalism, and reshape society in a socialist and communist direction.
- Withering Away of the State: the gradual disappearance of state and carceral institutions insofar as society becomes more equal and no longer requires them.
- Captive Maternal: not an identity, but a function undertaken by those most vulnerable to violence, war, poverty, police, and captivity who assume roles of caretaker, protest and movement maker, maroon, and war rebel.

Vladimir Lenin, *The State and Revolution* (1917)

1. The State: A Product of the Irreconcilability of Class Antagonisms

. . . in view of the unprecedently wide-spread distortion of Marxism, our prime task is to re-establish what Marx really taught on the subject of the state . . . the basic idea of Marxism with regard to the historical role and the meaning of the state [is that] the state is a product and a manifestation of the irreconcilability of class antagonisms. The state arises where, when and insofar as class antagonism objectively cannot be reconciled. And, conversely, the existence of the state proves that the class antagonisms are irreconcilable. . . .

According to Marx, the state is an organ of class rule, an organ for the oppression of one class by another; it is the creation of "order," which legalizes and perpetuates this oppression by moderating the conflict between classes . . . if the state is the product of the irreconcilability of class antagonisms, if it is a power standing above society and "alienating itself more and more from it," it is clear that the liberation of the oppressed class is impossible not only without a violent revolution, but also without the destruction of the apparatus of state power which was created by the ruling class and which is the embodiment of this "alienation". . . .

2. Special Bodies of Armed Men, Prisons, etc.

. . . Engels elucidates the concept of the "power" which is called the state, a power which arose from society but places itself above it and alienates itself more and more from it. What does this power mainly consist of? It consists of special bodies of armed men having prisons, etc., at their command. . . . A state arises, a special power is created, special bodies of armed men, and every revolution, by destroying the state apparatus, shows us the naked class struggle, clearly shows us how the ruling class strives to restore the special bodies of armed men which serve it, and how the oppressed class strives to create a new organization of this kind, capable of serving the exploited instead of the exploiters.

4. The "Withering Away" of the State, and Violent Revolution

Engels' words regarding the "withering away" of the state are so widely known, they are often quoted, and so clearly reveal the essence of the customary adaptation of Marxism to opportunism that we must deal with them in detail. We shall quote the whole argument from which they are taken.

> The proletariat seizes from state power and turns the means of production into state property to begin with. But thereby it abolishes itself as the proletariat, abolishes all class distinctions and class antagonisms, and abolishes also the state as state. Society thus far, operating amid class antagonisms, needed the state, that is, an organization of the particular exploiting class, for the maintenance of its external conditions of production, and, therefore, especially, for the purpose of forcibly keeping the exploited class in the conditions of oppression determined by the given mode of production (slavery, serfdom or bondage, wage-labor). The state was the official representative of society as a whole, its concentration in a visible corporation. But it was this only insofar as it was the state of that class which itself represented, for its own time, society as a whole: in ancient times, the state of slave-owning citizens; in the Middle Ages, of the feudal nobility; in our own time, of the bourgeoisie. When at last it becomes the real representative of the whole of society, it renders itself unnecessary. As soon as there is no longer any social class to be held in subjection, as soon as class rule, and the individual struggle for existence based upon the present

> anarchy in production, with the collisions and excesses arising from this struggle, are removed, nothing more remains to be held in subjection—nothing necessitating a special coercive force, a state. The first act by which the state really comes forward as the representative of the whole of society—the taking possession of the means of production in the name of society—is also its last independent act as a state. State interference in social relations becomes, in one domain after another, superfluous, and then dies down of itself. The government of persons is replaced by the administration of things, and by the conduct of processes of production. The state is not 'abolished.' It withers away. This gives the measure of the value of the phrase 'a free people's state,' both as to its justifiable use for a long time from an agitational point of view, and as to its ultimate scientific insufficiency; and also of the so-called anarchists' demand that the state be abolished overnight. . . .

It is safe to say that of this argument of Engels', which is so remarkably rich in ideas, only one point has become an integral part of socialist thought among modern socialist parties, namely, that according to Marx that state "withers away"—as distinct from the anarchist doctrine of the "abolition" of the state. . . . To prune Marxism to such an extent means reducing it to opportunism, for this "interpretation" only leaves a vague notion of a slow, even, gradual change, of absence of leaps and storms, of absence of revolution. The current, widespread, popular, if one may say so, conception of the "withering away" of the state undoubtedly means obscuring, if not repudiating, revolution. . . .

In the first place, at the very outset of his argument, Engels says that, in seizing state power, the proletariat thereby "abolishes the state as state" . . . these words briefly express the experience of one of the greatest proletarian revolutions, the Paris Commune of 1871. . . . As a matter of fact, Engels speaks here of the proletariat revolution "abolishing" the *bourgeois* state, while the words about the state withering away refer to the remnants of the *proletarian* state *after* the socialist revolution. According to Engels, the bourgeois state does not "wither away," but is "abolished" by the proletariat in the course of the revolution. What withers away after this revolution is the proletarian state or semi-state.

Secondly, the state is a "special coercive force." Engels gives this splendid and extremely profound definition here with the utmost lucidity. And from it follows that the "special coercive force" for the suppression of the proletariat by the bourgeoisie, of millions of working people by handfuls of the rich, must be replaced by a "special coercive force" for the suppression of the bourgeoisie by the proletariat (the dictatorship of the proletariat). This is precisely what is meant by "abolition of the state as state." This is precisely the "act" of taking possession of the means of production in the name of society. And it is self-evident that such a replacement of one (bourgeois) "special force" by another (proletarian) "special force" cannot possibly take place in the form of "withering away."

Thirdly, in speaking of the state "withering away," and the even more graphic and colorful "dying down of itself," Engels refers quite clearly and definitely to the period after "the state has taken possession of the means of production in the name of the whole of society," that is, after the socialist revolution. We all know that the political form of the "state" at that time is the most complete democracy. . . . Revolution alone can "abolish" the bourgeois state. The state in general, i.e., the most complete democracy, can only "wither away."

Fourthly, after formulating his famous proposition that "the state withers away," Engels at once explains specifically that this proposition is directed against both the opportunists and the anarchists.

In doing this, Engels puts in the forefront that conclusion, drawn from the proposition that "the state withers away," which is directed against the opportunists. . . .

We have already said above, and shall show more fully later, that the theory of Marx and Engels of the inevitability of a violent revolution refers to the bourgeois state. The latter cannot be superseded by the proletarian state (the dictatorship of the proletariat) through the process of "withering away," but, as a general rule, only through a violent revolution. . . . The necessity of systematically imbuing the masses with this and precisely this view of violent revolution lies at the root of the entire theory of Marx and Engels. . . . The supersession of the bourgeois state by the proletarian state is impossible without a violent revolution. The abolition of the proletarian state, i.e., of the state in general, is impossible except through the process of "withering away."

Walter Rodney, *How Europe Underdeveloped Africa* (1972)

From a political perspective, the period of transition from communalism to feudalism in Africa was one of state formation. At the beginning (and for many centuries), the state remained weak and immature. It acquired definite territorial boundaries, but inside those boundaries subjects lived in their own communities with scarcely any contact with the ruling class until the time came to pay an annual tax or tribute. Only when a group within the state refused to pay the tribute did the early African states mobilize their repressive machinery in the form of an army to demand what it considered as its rights from subjects. Slowly, various states acquired greater power over their many communities of citizens. They exacted corvée labor, they enlisted soldiers, and they appointed regular tax-collectors and local administrators. The areas of Africa in which labor relations were breaking out of communal restrictions corresponded to areas in which sophisticated political states were emerging. The rise of states was itself a form of development, which increased the scale of African politics and merged small ethnic groups into wider identities suggestive of nations.

In some ways, too much importance is attached to the growth of political states. It was in Europe that the nation state reached an advanced stage, and Europeans tended to use the presence or absence of well-organized polities as a measure of 'civilization.' That is not entirely justified, because in Africa there were small political units which had relatively advanced material and non-material cultures. For instance, neither the Ibo people of Nigeria nor the Kikuyu of Kenya ever produced large centralized governments in their traditional setting. But both had sophisticated systems of political rule based on clans and (in the case of the Ibo) on religious oracles and 'Secret Societies.' Both of them were efficient agriculturalists and iron workers, and the Ibo were manufacturing brass and bronze items ever since the nineth century A.D., if not earlier.

However, after making the above qualification, it can be conceded that on the whole the larger states in Africa had the most effective political structures and greater capacity for producing food, clothing, minerals and other material artefacts. It can readily be understood that those societies which had ruling classes were concerned with acquiring luxury and prestige items. The privileged groups in control of the state were keen to stimulate manufactures as well as to acquire them through trade. They were the ones that mobilized labor to produce a greater surplus above subsistence needs, and in the process they encouraged specialization and the division of labor.

Scholars often distinguish between groups in Africa which had states and those which were 'stateless.' Sometimes, the word stateless is carelessly or even abusively used; but it does describe those peoples who had no machinery of government coercion and no concept of a political unit wider than the family or the village. After all, if there is no class stratification in a society, it follows that there is no state, because the state arose as an instrument to be used by a particular class to control the rest of society in its own interests. Generally speaking, one can consider the stateless societies as among the older forms of sociopolitical organization in Africa, while the large states represented an evolution away from communalism—sometimes to the point of feudalism.

Joy James, *New Bones Abolition* (2023)

Black Feminists Can Be Captive Maternals, but It's Complicated

Feminism has no gender. To be a "feminist" is to advocate for equal rights and equity in resources for men and women (this would or should include trans wo/men and nonbinary people). If Black people lack equal rights and equity with (bourgeois) whites—and are not considered to actually be "human" and suffer disproportionate violence, severed natality, exploitation, and incarceration administered through the state and (vigilante) police forces—then this discussion is about more than gender. It is also about empire and colonialism, the ungendered and "queered" Black. The Captive Maternal as extension, companion, or alternative to Black feminisms is not inherently antagonistic to radical-central-liberal Black feminisms. Yet, unlike the majority of Black feminisms, the Captive Maternal is positioned as antagonist to the imperial state. Any form of state feminisms that promoted Black feminisms—from Hillary Clinton to Gloria Steinem—would also have to be critiqued in order to gain greater clarity. The Captive Maternal journey is rooted in war resistance. Those promoting a militarized state would never become allies of the Captive Maternal—they would become allies of liberalism and compradors. . . .

Black feminisms, in the plural, offer the capacity for progress, but its diverse destinations are driven by centrism, liberalism, radical liberalism (the most popular form of abolition), radicalism, and revolution. Black feminisms in conflict with Captive Maternal constructs are incubators for state feminism. Black feminisms could also be Captive Maternals. Given the varied forms of caretaking, Captive Maternals, even on the first stages of labor dedicated to home and social order, wield a function disciplined by strategy with interior emotional affects aligned with rebellion. Feminists are not inherently seeking rebellions against capitalism and colonialism. Captive Maternals acknowledge but do not always openly celebrate personal progress or gains under capitalism that largely accrue to (petite) bourgeois sectors. Captive Maternals intuitively or consciously understand that the entire system is a predatory mechanism. . . .

Captive Maternals resent and resist the theft or repurposing of their generative powers to stabilize state colonialism and police forces. . . . Captive Maternals intuit or scrutinize the inequality, dysfunction, and barbarity of power. . . . To scrutinize the stratified (dis) order of things requires stepping beyond personal trauma and grievances to see and confront structures. . . . Black feminisms aligned with state power boost one's individual or group ego to deflect from the fight to quell the state's predatory powers.

In the concentric circles of care, the dialectical spiral of struggle moves from caretaker, to protester, into movement maker, marronage, and war resister. . . . For the Captive Maternal, function is central. How we practice communal engagement with honor, and define "love" in a war zone, is pivotal for analyses and agency.

11 | POLICING & PRISONS TODAY

Study Questions:

1. What do police and prisons *do*? How do they serve capitalism?
2. What is the basis of police and prison power?
3. What kind of world needs police and prisons?
4. What kind of world *doesn't*?

Key Concepts:

– Pig Majority: all of those, Black and white, who do the work of the police without wearing the uniform, including vigilantes, elected officials, judges, juries, social workers, district attorneys, journalists, and individuals.

June Jordan, "Poem About Police Violence" (1978)

Tell me something
what you think would happen if
everytime they kill a black boy
then we kill a cop
everytime they kill a black man
then we kill a cop
you think the accident rate would lower subsequently?

sometimes the feeling like amaze me baby
comes back to my mouth and I am quiet
like Olympian pools from the running
mountainous snows under the sun

sometimes thinking about the 12th House of the Cosmos
or the way your ear ensnares the tip
of my tongue or signs that I have never seen
like DANGER WOMEN WORKING

I lose consciousness of ugly bestial rapid
and repetitive affront as when they tell me
18 cops in order to subdue one man
18 strangled him to death in the ensuing scuffle
(don't you idolize the diction of the powerful: subdue
and scuffle my oh my) and that the murder
that the killing of Arthur Miller on a Brooklyn
street was just a "justifiable accident" again
(Again)

People been having accidents all over the globe
so long like that I reckon that the only
suitable insurance is a gun
I'm saying war is not to understand or rerun
war is to be fought and won

sometimes the feeling like amaze me baby
blots it out/the bestial but
not too often tell me something
what you think would happen if
everytime they kill a black boy

then we kill a cop
everytime they kill a black man
then we kill a cop

you think the accident rate would lower subsequently

Geo Maher, *A World Without Police* (2021)

Policing and whiteness—white power—are inseparable. As W.E.B. Du Bois argued in Black Reconstruction, this has been true from the beginning, when "slavery demanded a special police force and such a force was made possible and unusually effective by the presence of the poor whites." As slave patrols morphed into police forces, moreover, little changed, and the "police system was arranged to deal with blacks alone, and tacitly assumed that every white man was ipso facto a member of that police."

After the abolition of slavery, when Black freedom threatened the plantation economy and terrified many whites, policing became more important, not less. "Black codes" across the South made Black labor mandatory under vagrancy laws, punishing those found in violation with forced labor. The objective was clear: to discipline a necessary workforce. Those who refused were imprisoned, and many were subjected to the regime of convict leasing—some of whom were returned in chains to the same plantations they had only just escaped. The broader result was a cheap labor force whose docility was ensured by the threat of re-enslavement, or worse. If policing disciplined former slaves, it provided concrete employment for many otherwise-destitute whites as overseers, slave breakers, and patrolmen. Whiteness, however, was not only about monetary wages, but also entailed what Du Bois called a "public and psychological wage" that "fed his vanity because it associated him with the masters." Poor whites were bestowed with symbolic superiority and titles, but also material privileges: access to public functions and parks, public education, and leniency in the courts.

These petty privileges and "wages of whiteness" encouraged poor whites to identify as white rather than as poor, ensuring their loyalty to their class enemies and disarming any potential solidarity with poor Black people, slave or free. The police were thus the linchpin holding together a vast, cross-class alliance that, for Du Bois, marked the tragedy of post-emancipation America. Poor whites had betrayed their own class interests by entering into a devil's bargain with their "race," thereby setting American capitalism on a path of untrammeled greed and racial avarice from which it hasn't strayed since. This racial bargain had upheld the slave system, and the same bargain would doom Reconstruction, a radical experiment in social and racial equality that had improved the lives of everyone, poor whites included, by breaking the political power of the planter class, abolishing debtors' prisons, establishing public schools, and eliminating property qualifications for voting.

Having chosen their race over their class, these ipso facto police took on another name: the Ku Klux Klan. Through terroristic intimidation, the Klan-police disenfranchised Black Southerners and imposed "a double system of justice" that sought "to use the courts as a means of re-enslaving the blacks." "Gradually," Du Bois wrote, "the whole white South became an armed and commissioned camp to keep Negroes in slavery and to kill the black rebel." The police stood against democracy from the very beginning, resisting with violent terror even its most limited representative form—one person, one vote. But this was in part because to grant basic suffrage to former slaves posed a threat to those limits and opened the door to more substantial demands. As Reconstruction governments showed, the vote was not an end in itself, but a means toward building that world of greater equality and more substantive participation that Du Bois called "abolition democracy." The Klan-police rolled back this ambitious vision, containing it within bounds acceptable for racists and capitalists alike.

While slave patrols provided the vicious blueprint, the policing of slaves in the South dovetailed with the policing of other "dangerous" classes like the poor and immigrant rabble of the North. It was in the context of Northern cities that professional policing had emerged in the United States, heavily influenced by the English model of Robert Peel's London Metropolitan Police. Even though their sources differed, there was no real contradiction between these two forms of policing—after all, in the development of American capitalism, slavery had been as important as industry, providing raw materials to the North and to London itself. In their genesis, police embodied the division of the poor, and in their practical function they uphold that division every day, patrolling the boundaries of property and that most peculiar form of property that is whiteness. American policing has always been about two things at once: controlling "dangerous" people and disciplining the workforce; assuaging the moral anxieties of white elites and the needs of capital accumulation; racist fear and economic profit.

Whether in the North or in the South, police have attacked workers and broken strikes, and they have policed the perceived vice and immorality that is primarily associated with people of color. After the abolition of slavery, policing helped keep the Black labor force on the plantations from which they had been momentarily freed, patrolling the boundaries of segregated neighborhoods for decades to come. And as deindustrialization set in in the 1970s and poor Black workers were pushed out of the labor market entirely, the police stepped in to enforce the violent feedback loop connecting ghettoes to prisons. This contemporary arrangement squeezes nearly free labor like blood from a stone, providing a never-ending stream of jobs for police and prison guards while protecting property—real estate values in particular—from the poorest. If Du Bois spoke more than a century ago of the role of the courts in re-enslaving Black people, the racist seeds of Jim Crow have borne fruit in the mass incarceration and the mass policing of today. How else to explain, more than a century after abolition, disparities in federal sentencing guidelines of one hundred to one between powder cocaine and crack?

It is no exaggeration to say that the South won the long Civil War, even if the fight rages on in the streets today. The racist policing pioneered under slavery and in the Jim Crow South have gone nationwide and metastasized—from Black codes to "broken windows," from convict leasing to the criminalization of Blackness. The watchword of American history is not change but continuity, not abolition but substitution. New structures of containment have replaced the old, in a seemingly interminable cycle driven by the irrepressible yearning of Black freedom dreams. Meanwhile, poor whites, dying of opioid addiction and preventable disease, choose the increasingly meager wages of whiteness over a better world for all, voting for more police as the coffers of the rich burst their hinges.

***

If whiteness were a job, it would be the police. But if policing emerged as historically indistinguishable from whiteness, and if white Americans continue to play a disproportionately heavy role in today's pig majority, what of the legions of Black and Brown police officers, commanders, and commissioners, district attorneys, mayors, and judges? What of the diversity among the ranks of border patrol, immigration and customs agents, and active duty foot soldiers of global imperialism abroad? And what of the complicity of the broader multiracial political class in what legal scholar James Forman Jr. has called "locking up our own?" . . . [I]n his groundbreaking sociological study The Philadelphia Negro, Du Bois himself documented how Black police officers had been appointed in the city as early as 1884. Almost exactly a century later in the same city, a Black mayor dropped a bomb on the MOVE Organization, burning down a city block and killing eleven—including several children—and a string of Black police commissioners have continued to this day to heap disproportionate brutality on poor people of color.

Policing is racist no matter who is doing the legwork. Even where intentions might be pure, racist fear is contagious, afflicting even officers of color, as repeated studies on implicit bias have demonstrated. More importantly, however, individual intentions matter little in the face of the structural racism of policing, which dispatches officers onto the streets to patrol the boundaries of whiteness and wealth, reinforcing and deepening racial and class inequalities in the process. And just as more Black police doesn't mean less racism, it's no solution to brutality either. . . .

Today's pig majority extends far beyond white people, but it is nonetheless fundamentally about white power. The presence of "Black faces in high places"—from the ranks of the police to political power—has done little to transform the deep structures of white supremacy in American society. What's more, they have actually provided the system with a powerful alibi, a Black mask for the perpetuation of white supremacy and capitalist exploitation—the spokespeople of the system and the storm troopers enforcing it. We live in a world of both Fergusons and Baltimores. But just as both names conjure the specter of police murder, they also bespeak a spirit of revolt among those who haven't been fooled by the post-racial hype.

Angela Davis, *Are Prisons Obsolete?* (2003)

The prison is not the only institution that has posed complex challenges to the people who have lived with it and have become so inured to its presence that they could not conceive of society without it. Within the history of the United States the system of slavery immediately comes to mind. Although as early as the American Revolution antislavery advocates promoted the elimination of African bondage, it took almost a century to achieve the abolition of the "peculiar institution." White antislavery abolitionists such as John Brown and William Lloyd Garrison were represented in the dominant media of the period as extremists and fanatics. When Frederick Douglass embarked on his career as an antislavery orator, white people—even those who were passionate abolitionists—refused to believe that a black slave could display such intelligence. The belief in the permanence of slavery was so widespread that even white abolitionists found it difficult to imagine black people as equals.

It took a long and violent civil war in order to legally disestablish the "peculiar institution." Even though the Thirteenth Amendment to the U.S. Constitution outlawed involuntary servitude, white supremacy continued to be embraced by vast numbers of people and became deeply inscribed in new institutions. One of these post-slavery institutions was lynching, which was widely accepted for many decades thereafter. Thanks to the work of figures such as Ida B. Wells, an antilynching campaign was gradually legitimized during the first half of the twentieth century. The NAACP, an organization that continues to conduct legal challenges against discrimination, evolved from these efforts to abolish lynching.

Segregation ruled the South until it was outlawed a century after the abolition of slavery. Many people who lived under Jim Crow could not envision a legal system defined by racial equality. . . . I have referred to these historical examples of efforts to dismantle racist institutions because they have considerable relevance to our discussion of prisons and prison abolition. It is true that slavery, lynching, and segregation acquired such a stalwart ideological quality that many, if not most, could not foresee their decline and collapse. Slavery, lynching, and segregation are certainly compelling examples of social institutions that, like the prison, were once considered to be as everlasting as the sun. Yet, in the case of all three examples, we can point to movements that assumed the radical stance of announcing the obsolescence of these institutions. . . .

What is the relationship between these historical expressions of racism and the role of the prison system today? Exploring such connections may offer us a different perspective on the current state of the punishment industry. . . . Are prisons racist institutions? Is racism so deeply entrenched in the institution of the prison that it is not possible to eliminate one without eliminating the other? These are questions that we should keep in mind as we examine the historical links between U.S. slavery and the early penitentiary system. The penitentiary as an institution that simultaneously punished and rehabilitated its inhabitants was a new system of punishment that first made its appearance in the United States around the time of the American Revolution. This new system was based on the replacement of capital and corporal punishment by incarceration.

Imprisonment itself was new neither to the United States nor to the world, but until the creation of this new institution called the penitentiary, it served as a prelude to punishment. People who were to be subjected to some form of corporal punishment were detained in prison until the execution of the punishment. With the penitentiary, incarceration became the punishment itself. As is indicated in the designation "penitentiary," imprisonment was regarded as rehabilitative and the penitentiary prison was devised to provide convicts with the conditions for reflecting on their crimes and, through penitence, for reshaping their habits and even their souls. Although some antislavery advocates spoke out against this new system of punishment during the revolutionary period, the penitentiary was generally viewed as a progressive reform, linked to the larger campaign for the rights of citizens.

In many ways, the penitentiary was a vast improvement over the many forms of capital and corporal punishment inherited from the English. However, the contention that prisoners would refashion themselves if only given the opportunity to reflect and labor in solitude and silence disregarded the impact of authoritarian regimes of living and work. Indeed, there were significant similarities between slavery and the penitentiary prison. . . .

Particularly in the United States, race has always played a central role in constructing presumptions of criminality. After the abolition of slavery, former slave states passed new legislation revising the Slave Codes in order to regulate the behavior of free blacks in ways similar to those that had existed during slavery. The new Black Codes proscribed a range of actions—such as vagrancy, absence from work, breach of job contracts, the possession of firearms, and insulting gestures or acts—that were criminalized only when the person charged was black. With the passage of the Thirteenth Amendment to the Constitution, slavery and involuntary servitude were putatively abolished. However, there was a significant exception. In the wording of the amendment, slavery and involuntary servitude were abolished "except as a punishment for crime, whereof the party shall have been duly convicted." According to the Black Codes, there were crimes defined by state law for which only black people could be "duly convicted." Thus, former slaves, who had recently been extricated from a condition of hard labor for life, could be legally sentenced to penal servitude.

In the immediate aftermath of slavery, the southern states hastened to develop a criminal justice system that could legally restrict the possibilities of freedom for newly released slaves. Black people became the prime targets of a developing convict lease system, referred to by many as a reincarnation of slavery. The Mississippi Black Codes, for example, declared vagrant anyone who was guilty of theft, had run away [from a job, apparently], was drunk, was wanton in conduct or speech, had neglected job or family, handled money carelessly, and ... all other idle and disorderly persons." Thus, vagrancy was coded as a black crime, one punishable by incarceration and forced labor, sometimes on the very plantations that previously had thrived on slave labor. . . .

Slave owners may have been concerned for the survival of individual slaves, who, after all, represented significant investments. Convicts, on the other hand, were leased not as individuals, but as a group, and they could be worked literally to death without affecting the profitability of a convict crew. According to descriptions by contemporaries, the conditions under which leased convicts and county chain gangs lived were far worse than those under which black people had lived as slaves. Alex Lichtenstein, whose study focuses on the role of the convict lease system in forging a new labor force for the South, identifies the lease system, along with the new Jim Crow laws, as the central institution in the development of a racial state.

> New South capitalists in Georgia and elsewhere were able to use the state to recruit and discipline a convict labor force, and thus were able to develop their states' resources without creating a wage labor force, and without undermining planters' control of black labor. In fact, quite the opposite: the penal system could be used as a powerful sanction against rural blacks who challenged the racial order upon which agricultural labor control relied.

Lichtenstein discloses, for example, the extent to which the building of Georgia railroads during the nineteenth century relied on black convict labor. . . . Lichtenstein's major argument is that the convict lease was not an irrational regression; it was not primarily a throwback to pre-capitalist modes of production. Rather, it was a most efficient and most rational deployment of racist strategies to swiftly achieve industrialization in the South.

The persistence of the prison as the main form of punishment, with its racist and sexist dimensions, has created this historical continuity between the nineteenth- and early twentieth-century convict lease system and the privatized prison business today. While the convict lease system was legally abolished, its structures of exploitation have reemerged in the patterns of privatization, and, more generally, in the wide-ranging corporatization of punishment that has produced a prison industrial complex.

It is ironic that the prison itself was a product of concerted efforts by reformers to create a better system of punishment. If the words "prison reform" so easily slip from our lips, it is because "prison" and "reform" have been inextricably linked since the beginning of the use of imprisonment as the main means of punishing those who violate social norms. As I have already indicated, the origins of the prison are associated with the American Revolution and therefore with the resistance to the colonial power of England. Today this seems ironic, but incarceration within a penitentiary was assumed to be humane—at least far more humane than the capital and corporal punishment inherited from England and other European countries. . . . Red-hot pincers were used to burn away the flesh from his limbs, and molten lead, boiling oil, burning resin, and other substances were melted together and poured onto the wounds. Finally, he was drawn and quartered, his body burned, and the ashes tossed into the wind. Under English common law, a conviction for sodomy led to the punishment of being buried alive, and convicted heretics also were burned alive. . . .

European and American reformers set out to end macabre penalties such as this, as well as other forms of corporal punishment such as the stocks and pillories, whippings, brandings, and amputations. Prior to the appearance of punitive incarceration, such punishment was designed to have its most profound effect not so much on the person punished as on the crowd of spectators. Punishment was, in essence, public spectacle. Reformers such as John Howard in England and Benjamin Rush in Pennsylvania argued that punishment—if carried out in isolation, behind the walls of the prison—would cease to be revenge and would actually reform those who had broken the law.

It should also be pointed out that punishment has not been without its gendered dimensions. Women were often punished within the domestic domain, and instruments of torture were sometimes imported by authorities into the household. In seventeenth-century Britain, women whose husbands identified them as quarrelsome and un-accepting of male dominance were punished by means of a gossip's bridle, or "branks," a headpiece with a chain attached and an iron bit that was introduced into the woman's mouth. Although the branking of women was often linked to a public parade, this contraption was sometimes hooked to a wall of the house, where the punished woman remained until her husband decided to release her. I mention these forms of punishment inflicted on women because, like the punishment inflicted on slaves, they were rarely taken up by prison reformers.

Thus far I have largely used gender-neutral language to describe the historical development of the prison and its reformers. But convicts punished by imprisonment in emergent penitentiary systems were primarily male. This reflected the deeply gender-biased structure of legal, political, and economic rights. Since women were largely denied public status as rights-bearing individuals, they could not be easily punished by the deprivation of such rights through imprisonment. This was especially true of married women, who had no standing before the law. According to English common law, marriage resulted in a state of "civil death," as symbolized by the wife's assumption of the husband's name. Consequently, she tended to be punished for revolting against her domestic duties rather than for failure in her meager public responsibilities. The relegation of white women to domestic economies prevented them from playing a significant role in the emergent commodity realm. This was especially true since wage labor was typically gendered as male and racialized as white. It is not fortuitous that domestic corporal punishment for women survived long after these modes of punishment had become obsolete for (white) men. The persistence of domestic violence painfully attests to these historical modes of gendered punishment. . . .

I have highlighted the similarities between the early U.S. penitentiary—with its aspirations toward individual rehabilitation—and the repressive supermaxes of our era as a reminder of the mutability of history. What was once regarded as progressive and even revolutionary represents today the marriage of technological superiority and political backwardness. No one—not even the most ardent defenders of the supermax—would try to argue today that absolute segregation, including sensory deprivation, is restorative and healing. The prevailing justification for the supermax is that the horrors it creates are the perfect complement for the horrifying personalities deemed the worst of the worst by the prison system. In other words, there is no pretense that rights are respected, there is no concern for the individual, there is no sense that men and women incarcerated in supermaxes deserve anything approaching respect and comfort. . . .

Mumia Abu-Jamal, who has challenged the contemporary dismantling of prison education programs, asks in *Live from Death Row*,

> What societal interest is served by prisoners who remain illiterate? What social benefit is there in ignorance? How are people corrected while imprisoned if their education is outlawed? Who profits (other than the prison establishment itself) from stupid prisoners?

A practicing journalist before his arrest in 1982 on charges of killing Philadelphia policeman Daniel Faulkner, Abu Jamal has regularly produced articles on capital punishment, focusing especially on its racial and class disproportions. His ideas have helped to link critiques of the death penalty with the more general challenges to the expanding U.S. prison system and are particularly helpful to activists who seek to associate death penalty abolitionism with prison abolitionism. . . . Abu-Jamal and many other prison writers have strongly criticized the prohibition of Pell Grants for prisoners, which was enacted in the 1994 crime bill, as indicative of the contemporary pattern of dismantling educational programs behind bars. . . .

It should also be kept in mind that until the abolition of slavery, the vast majority of black women were subject to regimes of punishment that differed significantly from those experienced by white women. As slaves, they were directly and often brutally disciplined for conduct considered perfectly normal in a context of freedom. Slave punishment was visibly gendered—special penalties, were, for example, reserved for pregnant women unable to reach the quotas that determined how long and how fast they should work. . . . If we expand our definition of punishment under slavery, we can say that the coerced sexual relations between slave and master constituted a penalty exacted on women, if only for the sole reason that they were slaves. In other words, the deviance of the slave master was transferred to the slave woman, whom he victimized. Likewise, sexual abuse by prison guards is translated into hyper-sexuality of women prisoners. . . .

The exploitation of prison labor by private corporations is one aspect among an array of relationships linking corporations, government, correctional communities, and media. These relationships constitute what we now call a prison industrial complex. The term "prison industrial complex" was introduced by activists and scholars to contest prevailing beliefs that increased levels of crime were the root cause of mounting prison populations. Instead, they argued, prison construction and the attendant drive to fill these new structures with human bodies have been driven by ideologies of racism and the pursuit of profit. . . .

A more cogent way to define the relationship between the military industrial complex and the prison industrial complex would be to call it symbiotic. These two complexes mutually support and promote each other and, in fact, often share technologies. During the early nineties, when defense production was temporarily on the decline, this connection between the military industry and the criminal justice/punishment industry was acknowledged in a 1994 *Wall Street Journal* article. . . .

> Parts of the defense establishment are cashing in, too, sensing a logical new line of business to help them offset military cutbacks. Westinghouse Electric Corp., Minnesota Mining and Manufacturing Co, GDE Systems (a division of the old General Dynamics) and Alliant Techsystems Inc., for instance, are pushing crime fighting equipment and have created special divisions to retool their defense technology for America's streets. . . .

It was during the decade of the 1980s that corporate ties to the punishment system became more extensive and entrenched than ever before. But throughout the history of the U.S. prison system, prisoners have always constituted a potential source of profit. For example, they have served as valuable subjects in medical research, thus positioning the prison as a major link between universities and corporations. . . .

In the context of an economy that was driven by an unprecedented pursuit of profit, no matter what the human cost, and the concomitant dismantling of the welfare state, poor people's abilities to survive became increasingly constrained by the looming presence of the prison. The massive prison-building project that began in the 1980s created the means of concentrating and managing what the capitalist system had implicitly declared to be a human surplus. In the meantime, elected officials and the dominant media justified the new draconian sentencing practices, sending more and more people to prison in the frenzied drive to build more and more prisons by arguing that this was the only way to make our communities safe from murderers, rapists, and robbers. . . . During the same period when crime rates were declining, prison populations soared. . . .

The prison industrial complex is fueled by privatization patterns that, it will be recalled, have also drastically transformed health care, education, and other areas of our lives. Moreover, the prison privatization trends—both the increasing presence of corporations in the prison economy and the establishment of private prisons—are reminiscent of the historical efforts to create a profitable punishment industry based on the new supply of "free" black male laborers in the aftermath of the Civil War. . . . The privatization characteristic of convict leasing has its contemporary parallels, as companies such as CCA and Wackenhut literally run prisons for profit. . . .

Extensive corporate investment in prisons has significantly raised the stakes for antiprison work. It means that serious antiprison activists must be willing to look much further in their analyses and organizing strategies than the actual institution of the prison. Prison reform rhetoric, which has always undergirded dominant critiques of the prison system, will not work in this new situation. If reform approaches have tended to bolster the permanence of the prison in the past, they certainly will not suffice to challenge the economic and political relationships that sustain the prison today. This means that in the era of the prison industrial complex, activists must pose hard questions about the relationship between global capitalism and the spread of U.S.-style prisons throughout the world.

The global prison economy is indisputably dominated by the United States. This economy not only consists of the products, services, and ideas that are directly marketed to other governments, but it also exercises an enormous influence over the development of the style of state punishment throughout the world. . . . The uncontested detention of increasing numbers of undocumented immigrants from the global South has been aided considerably by the structures and ideologies associated with the prison industrial complex. We can hardly move in the direction of justice and equality in the twenty-first century if we are unwilling to recognize the enormous role played by this system in extending the power of racism and xenophobia.

Radical opposition to the global prison industrial complex sees the antiprison movement as a vital means of expanding the terrain on which the quest for democracy will unfold. This movement is thus antiracist, anticapitalist, antisexist, and antihomophobic. It calls for the abolition of the prison as the dominant mode of punishment but at the same time recognizes the need for genuine solidarity with the millions of men, women, and children who are behind bars. A major challenge of this movement is to do the work that will create more humane, habitable environments for people in prison without bolstering the permanence of the prison system. How, then, do we accomplish this balancing act of passionately attending to the needs of prisoners—calling for less violent conditions, an end to state sexual assault, improved physical and mental health care, greater access to drug programs, better educational work opportunities, unionization of prison labor, more connections with families and communities, shorter or alternative sentencing and at the same time call for alternatives to sentencing altogether, no more prison construction, and abolitionist strategies that question the place of the prison in our future?

Assata Shakur, "Women in Prison: How We Are" (1978)

There are no criminals here at Riker's Island Correctional Institution for Women, (New York), only victims. Most of the women (over 95 percent) are black and Puerto Rican. Many were abused children. Most have been abused by men and all have been abused by "the system."

There are no big-time gangsters here, no premeditated mass murderers, no godmothers. There are no big-time dope dealers, no kidnappers, no Watergate women. There are virtually no women here charged with white collar crimes like embezzling or fraud. Most of the women have drug related cases. Many are charged as accessories to crimes committed by men. The major crimes that women here are charged with are prostitution, pick-pocketing, shop lifting, robbery and drugs. Women who have prostitution cases or who are doing "fine" time make up a substantial part of the short-term population. The women see stealing or hustling as necessary for the survival of themselves or their children because jobs are scarce, and welfare is impossible to live on. One thing is clear: amerikan capitalism is in no way threatened by the women in prison on Riker's Island. . . .

The guards have successfully convinced most of the women that Riker's Island is a country club. They say that it is a playhouse compared to some other prisons (especially male): a statement whose partial veracity is not predicated upon the humanity of correction officials at Riker's Island, but, rather, by contrast to the unbelievably barbaric conditions of other prisons. Many women are convinced that they are, somehow, "getting over." Some go so far as to reason that because they are not doing hard time, they aren't really in prison.

This image is further reinforced the pseudo-motherly attitude of many of the guards; a deception which all too often successfully reverts women into children. The guards call the women inmates by their first names. . . . But beneath the motherly veneer, the reality of guard life is every present. Most of the guards are black, usually from working class, upward bound, civil service-oriented backgrounds. They identify with the middle class, have middle class values and are extremely materialistic. They are not the most intelligent women in the world and many are extremely limited.

Most are aware that there is no justice in the amerikan judicial system and that blacks and Puerto Ricans are discriminated against in every facet of amerikan life. But, at the same time, they are convinced that the system is somehow "lenient." To them, the women in prison are "losers" who don't have enough sense to stay out of jail. Most believe in the boot strap theory—anybody can "make it" if they try hard enough. They congratulate themselves on their great accomplishments. In contrast to themselves they see the inmate as ignorant, uncultured, self-destructive, weak-minded and stupid. They ignore the fact that their dubious accomplishments are not based on superior intelligence or effort, but only on chance and a civil service list.

Many guards hate and feel trapped by their jobs. The guard is exposed to a certain amount of abuse from co-workers, from the brass as well as from inmates, ass kissing, robotizing and mandatory overtime. (It is common practice for guards to work a double shift at least once a week.) But no matter how much they hate the military structure, the infighting, the ugliness of their tasks, they are very aware of how close they are to the welfare lines. If they were not working as guards most would be underpaid or unemployed. Many would miss the feeling of superiority and power as much as they would miss the money, especially the cruel, sadistic ones. The guards are usually defensive about their jobs and indicate by their behavior that they are not at all free from guilt. They repeatedly, compulsively say, as if to convince themselves, "This is a job just like any other job." The more they say it the more preposterous it seems.

The major topic of conversation here is drugs. Eighty percent of inmates have used drugs when they were in the street. Getting high is usually the first thing a woman says she's going to do when she gets out. In prison, as on the streets, an escapist culture prevails. At least 50 percent of the prison population take some form of psychotropic drug. Elaborate schemes to obtain contraband drugs are always in the works.

Days are spent in pleasant distractions: soap operas, prison love affairs, card playing and game playing. A tiny minority are seriously involved in academic pursuits or the learning of skills. An even smaller minority attempt to study available law books. There are no jail house lawyers and most of the women lack knowledge of even the most rudimentary legal procedures. When asked what happened in court, or, what their lawyers said, they either don't know or don't remember. Feeling totally helpless and totally railroaded a woman will curse out her lawyer or the judge with little knowledge of what is being done or of what should be done. Most plead guilty, whether they are guilty or not. The few who do go to trial usually have lawyers appointed by the state and usually are convicted.

Here, the word lesbian seldom, if ever, is mentioned. Most, if not all, of the homosexual relationships here involve role playing. The majority of relationships are either asexual or semi-sexual. The absence of sexual consummation is only partially explained by prison prohibition against any kind of sexual behavior. Basically the women are not looking for sex. They are looking for love, for concern and companionship. For relief from the overwhelming sense of isolation and solitude that pervades each of us.

Women who are "aggressive" or who play the masculine roles are referred to as butches, bulldaggers or stud broads. They are always in demand because they are always in the minority. Women who are "passive," or who play feminine roles are referred to as fems. The butch-fem relationships are often oppressive, resembling the most oppressive, exploitative aspect of a sexist society. It is typical to hear butches threatening fems with physical violence and it is not uncommon for butches to actually beat their "women." Some butches consider themselves pimps and go with the women who have the most commissary, the most contraband or the best outside connections. They feel they are a class above ordinary women which entitles them to "respect." They dictate to fems what they are to do and many insist the fems wash, iron, sew and clean their cells for them. A butch will refer to another butch as "man." A butch who is well liked is known as "one of the fellas" by her peers.

Once in prison changes in roles are common. Many women who are strictly heterosexual in the street become butch in prison. "Fems" often create butches by convincing an inmate that she would make a "cute butch." About 80 percent of the prison population engage in some form of homosexual relationship. Almost all follow negative, stereotypic male/ female role models. There is no connection between the women's movement and lesbianism. Most of the women at Riker's Island have no idea what feminism is, let alone lesbianism. Feminism, the women's liberation movement and the gay liberation movement are worlds away from women at Riker's.

The black liberation struggle is equally removed from the lives of women at Riker's. While they verbalize acute recognition that amerika is a racist country where the poor are treated like dirt they, nevertheless, feel responsible for the filth of their lives. The air at Riker's is permeated with self-hatred. Many women bear marks on their arms, legs and wrists from suicide attempts or self-mutilation. They speak about themselves in self-deprecating terms. They consider themselves failures.

While most women contend that whitey is responsible for their oppression they do not examine the cause or source of that oppression. There is no sense of class struggle. They have no sense of communism, no definition of it, but they consider it a bad thing. They do not want to destroy Rockefella. They want to be like him. . . . Politicians are considered liars and crooks. The police are hated. Yet, during cop and robber movies, some cheer loudly for the cops. . . . A striking difference between women and men prisoners at Riker's Island is the absence of revolutionary rhetoric among the women. We have no study groups. We have no revolutionary literature around. There are no groups of militants attempting to "get their heads together." The women at Riker's seem vaguely aware of what a revolution is but generally regard it as an impossible dream. Not at all practical.

While men in prison struggle to maintain their manhood there is no comparable struggle by women to preserve their womanhood. One frequently hears women say, "Put a bunch of bitches together and you've got nothin but trouble"; and, "Women don't stick together, that's why we don't have nothin." Men prisoners constantly refer to each other as brother. Women prisoners rarely refer to each other as sister. Instead, "bitch" and "whore" are the common terms of reference. Women, however, are much kinder to each other than men, and any form of violence other than a fist fight is virtually unknown. Rape, murder and stabbings at the women's prison are non-existent.

For many, prison is not that much different from the street. It is, for some, a place to rest and recuperate. For the prostitute prison is a vacation from turning tricks in the rain and snow. A vacation from brutal pimps. Prison for the addict is a place to get clean, get medical work done and gain weight. Often, when the habit becomes too expensive, the addict gets herself busted, (usually subconsciously) so she can get back in shape, leave with a clean system ready to start all over again. One woman claims that for a month or two every year she either goes jail or to the crazy house to get away from her husband.

For many the cells are not much different from the tenements, the shooting galleries and the welfare hotels they live in on the street. Sick call is no different from the clinic or the hospital emergency room. The fights are the same except they are less dangerous. The police are the same. The poverty is the same. The alienation is the same. The racism is the same. The sexism is the same. The drugs are the same and the system is the same. Riker's is just another institution. In childhood school was their prison, or youth houses or reform schools or children shelters or foster homes or mental hospitals or drug programs and they see all institutions as indifferent to their needs, yet necessary to their survival.

The women at Riker's Island come there from places like Harlem, Brownsville, Bedford-Stuyvesant, South Bronx and South Jamaica. They come from places where dreams have been abandoned like the buildings. Where there is no more sense of community. Where neighborhoods are transient. Where isolated people run from one fire trap to another. The cities have removed us from our strengths, from our roots, from our traditions. They have taken away our gardens and our sweet potato pies and given us McDonald's. They have become our prisons, locking us into the futility and decay of pissy hallways that lead nowhere. They have alienated us from each other and made us fear each other. They have given us dope and television as a culture. . . .

What of our Past? What of our History? What of our Future?

I can imagine the pain and the strength of my great great grandmothers who were slaves and my great great grandmothers who were Cherokee Indians trapped on reservations. I remembered my great grandmother who walked everywhere rather than sit in the back of the bus. I think about North Carolina and my hometown and i remember the women of my grandmother's generation: strong, fierce women who could stop you with a look out the corners of their eyes. Women who walked with majesty; who could wring a chicken's neck and scale a fish. Who could pick cotton, plant a garden and sew without a pattern. Women who boiled clothes white in big black cauldrons and who hummed work songs and lullabys. Women who visited the elderly, made soup for the sick and shortnin bread for the babies.

Women who delivered babies, searched for healing roots and brewed medicines. Women who darned sox and chopped wood and layed bricks. Women who could swim rivers and shoot the head off a snake. Women who took passionate responsibility for their children and for their neighbors' children too. The women in my grandmother's generation made giving an art form. "Here, gal, take this pot of collards to Sister Sue"; "Take this bag of pecans to school for the teacher"; "Stay here while I go tend Mister Johnson's leg." Every child in the neighborhood ate in their kitchens. They called each other sister because of feeling rather than as the result of a movement. They supported each other through the lean times, sharing the little they had.

The women of my grandmother's generation in my hometown trained their daughters for womanhood. They taught them to give respect and to demand respect. They taught their daughters how to churn butter; how to use elbow grease. They taught their daughters to respect the strength of their bodies, to lift boulders and how to kill a hog; what to do for colic, how to break a fever and how to make a poultice, patchwork quilts, plait hair and how to hum and sing. They taught their daughters to take care, to take charge and to take responsibility. They would not tolerate a "lazy heifer" or a "gal with her head in the clouds." Their daughters had to learn how to get their lessons, how to survive, how to be strong. The women of my grandmother's generation were the glue that held family and the community together. They were the backbone of the church. And of the school. They regarded outside institutions with dislike and distrust. They were determined that their children should survive and they were committed to a better future.

I think about my sisters in the movement. I remember the days when, draped in African garb, we rejected our foremothers and ourselves as castrators. We did penance for robbing the brother of his manhood, as if we were the oppressor. I remember the days of the Panther Party when we were "moderately liberated." When we were allowed to wear pants and expected to pick up the gun. The days when we gave doe-eyed looks to our leaders. The days when we worked like dogs and struggled desperately for the respect which they struggled desperately not to give us. I remember the black history classes that did mention women and the posters of our "leaders" where women were conspicuously absent. We visited our sisters who bore the complete responsibility of the children while the Brotha was doing his thing. Or had moved on to bigger and better things.

Most of us rejected the white women's movement. Miss ann was still Miss ann to us whether she burned her bras or not. We could not muster sympathy for the fact that she was trapped in her mansion and oppressed by her husband. We were, and still are, in a much more terrible jail. We knew that our experiences as black women were completely different from those of our sisters in the white women's movement. And we had no desire to sit in some consciousness raising group with white women and bare our souls.

Women can never be free in a country that is not free. We can never be liberated in a country where the institutions that control our lives are oppressive. We can never be free while our men are oppressed. Or while the amerikan government and amerikan capitalism remain intact. But it is imperative to our struggle that we build a strong black women's movement. It is imperative that we, as black women, talk about the experiences that shaped us; that we assess our strengths and weaknesses and define our own history. It is imperative that we discuss positive ways to teach and socialize our children.

The poison and pollution of capitalist cities is choking us. We need the strong medicine of our foremothers to make us well again. We need their medicines to give us strength to fight and the drive to win. Under the guidance of Harriet Tubman and Fannie Lou Hamer and all of our foremothers, let us rebuild a sense of community. Let us rebuild the culture of giving and carry on the tradition of fierce determination to move on closer to freedom.

12 | ABOLITION & RECONSTRUCTION TODAY

Study Questions:

1. What does abolition mean today? What does it mean to *us*?
2. What does a reconstructed city, country, and globe look like?
3. What campaigns in the present or future point toward abolition & reconstruction?

Key Concepts:

- Reformist Reforms vs. Non-Reformist Reforms: reformist reforms help to preserve the existing carceral system by upholding and legitimizing the power of police and prisons, whereas non-reformist (or even abolitionist) reforms are those changes that help weaken carceral power and point toward a new world.
- The "Attrition Model": a long-range strategy for abolition that involves the wearing down of the carceral system through a) *moratorium*, halting prison construction, b) *decarceration*, getting people released from prison, and c) *excarceration*, preventing people from going to prison in the first place.
- Nonprofit Industrial Complex: the way that nonprofit organizations function as a kind of "soft power" to maintain the status quo by connecting wealthy capitalists to charitable causes that co-opt, buy off, and undermine popular power and resistance.

Mariame Kaba, "Police 'Reforms' You Should Always Oppose" (2014)

Here is a simple guide for evaluating any suggested "reforms" of U.S. policing in this historical moment.

1. Are the proposed reforms allocating more money to the police? If yes, then you should oppose them.
2. Are the proposed reforms advocating for MORE police and policing (under euphemistic terms like "community policing" run out of regular police districts)? If yes, then you should oppose them.
3. Are the proposed reforms primarily technology-focused? If yes, then you should oppose them because:
   a. It means more money to the police.
   b. Said technology is more likely to be turned against the public than it is to be used against cops.
   c. Police violence won't end through technological advances (no matter what someone is selling you).
4. Are the proposed "reforms" focused on individual dialogues with individual cops? And will these "dialogues" be funded with tax dollars? I am never against dialogue. It's good to talk with people. These conversations, however, should not be funded by taxpayer money. That money is better spent elsewhere. Additionally, violence is endemic to U.S. policing itself. There are some nice individual people who work in police departments. I've met some of them. But individual dialogue projects reinforce the "bad apples" theory of oppressive policing. This is not a problem of individually terrible officers rather it is a problem of a corrupt and oppressive policing system built on controlling and managing the marginalized while protecting property.

What "reforms" should you support (in the interim) then?

1. Proposals and legislation to offer reparations to victims of police violence and their families.
2. Proposals and legislation to require police officers to carry personal liability insurance to cover costs of brutality or death claims.
3. Proposals and legislation to decrease and redirect policing and prison funds to other social goods.
4. Proposals and legislation for (elected) independent civilian police accountability boards with power to investigate, discipline, fire police officers and administrators. [WITH SOME SERIOUS CAVEATS]
5. Proposals and legislation to disarm the police.
6. Proposals to simplify the process of dissolving existing police departments.
7. Proposals and legislation for data transparency (stops, arrests, budgeting, weapons, etc.)

Ultimately, the only way that we will address oppressive policing is to abolish the police. Therefore all of the "reforms" that focus on strengthening the police or "morphing" policing into something more invisible but still as deadly should be opposed.

Dean Spade, "No Cops, Courts, or Cages Means No State" (2023)

Police, prisons, borders, and militaries are co-constitutive with the state form, and the authority of the state cannot be maintained without them. In a recent episode of The Dig on abolition with Geo Maher and Mariame Kaba, Kaba described state function as the capacity to "protect and redistribute." What contemporary states protect are private property relations which make it possible for a small elite to extract from most people and the planet. They redistribute wealth upward, concentrate it and protect that concentration from attacks by the people from whom it was extracted. Even communist and socialist countries have been organized to facilitate this domination and extraction for elite interests.

Some on the left believe that states could become caregiving by redistributing money downward and protecting people from harms of elite-serving systems. For example, some think the government will protect us from pollution, poisoning, and labor-abuse through regulation. However, in the United States, government regulations merely establish *how much* each industry can exploit, poison, and pollute, while insulating bosses, landlords, and industry from liability and preventing us from stopping these harms. For example, workers' compensation benefits, are designed not to ensure that workers get the care they need when injured on the job but to limit how much redress workers can seek after being harmed by dangerous conditions. Another example is California's AB 1054, passed after the utility company PG&E caused the deadly and devastating Camp Fire in 2018. AB 1054 protects PG&E from liability for the fire, allowing the company to continue its negligent operations.

Or consider how the court system regulates the relationship between landlords and tenants, workers and owners, forcing tenants and workers to fruitlessly pursue (often at great risk) individual claims through rigged procedures where wealthy judges determine outcomes and bosses and landlords write the laws. "Housing rights" and "workers' rights" regulations are designed to redirect people away from collective action that works better to win justice, such as labor and rent strikes, rural and urban land and factory takeovers, fighting the cops to stop eviction attempts, and squatting. State regulation does not protect people from owners, bosses, and landlords but facilitates their domination and regulates people, limiting how we can resist. Regulation is used to protect extraction and keep people subject to it, such as by creating and enforcing immigration statuses to keep some workers especially exploitable or creating licensure schemes that prevent us from organizing health and care projects outside of racist, ableist and patriarchal care industries. Health care licensure and insurance schemes, for example, ensure profits for the health care industry and make many forms of community-based care illegal, such that mutual aid projects providing medicine, counseling, or other basic care face criminalization.

Some people also believe that through taxation, the state can redistribute wealth and reduce inequality. However, taxation primarily collects money for military and criminalization apparatuses to control people and facilitate extraction, not to support well-being. State infrastructure projects are overwhelmingly used to support white life and white property values and displace and poison non-elites. The state form developed with and through racial capitalism and its very purpose is to protect and sustain private property relations that make people exploitable, make almost everything for profit, and prevent people from meeting our own needs. The technologies of domination that have created the drastic material inequality under which we live are what produce and maintain state and corporate power, wealth concentration, and ecological crisis. When governments appear to redistribute wealth downward, it is almost always a temporary concession to quell dissent and stabilize the status quo. Governments are functioning exactly as designed, with flexibility and responsiveness to keep the scheme running.

I will focus on my experiences being a poverty lawyer and abolitionist in a U.S. context, although many theorists suggest these arguments can be applied more broadly. As a settler colonial, racial project established through chattel slavery and genocide, it's particularly difficult to imagine the U.S. government as a site of caregiving. Feminist, anti-racist, and disability justice movements have consistently demonstrated that care programs like welfare and social services police and punish marginalized groups and sort people in crisis into hierarchies of deservingness that justify stigma, abandonment, and premature death. Care systems often expand to respond to uprisings but quickly recede when elites regain control. The benefits and schemes they create are revocable and conditional and carefully crafted to exclude stigmatized populations. Feminist and disability justice insights about the problems of state violence masquerading as care, such as in welfare, disability benefits, and family policing systems, are crucial for abolitionists as our opponents respond to critiques with new proposals for "softer" interventions, from police social workers to electronic home monitoring schemes to supposedly feminist jails.

US history and contemporary conditions provide fertile ground for exploring these themes. We can also study how states formed and developed by reading scholars like Peter Kropotkin, Peter Gelderloos, Dilar Dirik, and Modibo Kadalie who ask these larger questions. Their work suggests that states are created when an elite conquers a territory, draws borders, invents external and internal enemies through racialization and gendering processes that invent populations to be cultivated and populations to be abandoned, and legitimizes practices by which people are ruled by people they don't know. Creating states requires preventing people from accessing collective capacities for reproduction and survival and rerouting them through a system designed to benefit elite interests. We can see this today in forced participation in a for-profit-wage economy to meet our basic needs, or coerced dependence on the criminalization system for safety even as it supports the wealth-concentrating arrangements that endanger our lives. It has taken a long time to create this arrangement of domination and extraction, and people have always resisted it creatively and relentlessly.

Resistance movements often call for collective self-determination—making decisions about our food, transportation, health, education, and energy systems, how we understand harm and cultivate safety ourselves. We want to be able to decide to power our communities and build food systems ourselves without fossil fuels, to block new prisons, dams, mines, or pipelines, to move without borders, to never be taxed for war and cops. The many crises we face, created by governments that control us on behalf of the elites that control them, require real solutions. These solutions will not be generated by the same entity that created the crises.

Does it matter? Can we work on abolition even if we disagree about taking over or getting rid of these governments? We can, up to a point. We can do anti-expansion and dismantling campaigns, support criminalized people and build mutual aid projects. But disagreement will influence our approach to the work—for example, with regard to time and resources given to electoral campaigns or to the amount of faith we have in the "invest" part of invest/divest defund tactics. Those who believe state capacity can turn toward well-being might see more potential for winning housing, childcare, healthcare, or income support through budget shifts. Others might see the invest/divest strategy as a chance to shrink the carceral apparatus, knowing we can gain concessions that reduce suffering, even if temporarily for a limited number of people in conditional and revocable ways, and recruit more people to abolitionist mobilizations. We might take up invest work as an experiment to see what we can get from the budget in the short term, knowing that the system of profit extraction, taxation, and spending cannot build vitally needed beneficial infrastructure for reproducing our lives.

Others might see the invest/divest strategy as perpetuating the fantasy of a caregiving state, misdirecting efforts away from building autonomous survival infrastructure. They might be wary of non-profitization when imagining the outcomes of invest work, aware that budget reallocations for survival needs will, at best, be funneled to non-profits which siphon off overhead expenses, distribute necessities in ways that perpetuate exclusions and stigma, and are limited by philanthropic control. Non-profit governance and stewardship of human needs is insufficiently distinct from government or corporate rule, and fail to create more participatory ways of creating and sustaining what people need to survive.

Disagreement about getting rid of or taking over the state can also impact movement culture and tactics. Often, those interested in seizing the state are more likely to limit dissent, whereas those interested in eliminating governments tend to endorse disobedience, disruption, and attack. Historically, disruption is what makes change; condoned dissent is absorbed and stabilizes and perpetuates the systems that produce crises.

What happens if we apply abolitionist analysis of police and prisons to the state form? What abolitionists believe about cops and cages also holds for government:

- Built for domination, control, and extraction, not to keep us safe
- Serves elite interests, masquerades as belonging to the people
- Is actually working exactly as designed so tinkering or "fixing" is futile
- Fantasies of it becoming caring prevent us from addressing its harms
- People fear chaos, violence, and mayhem without it, yet we know that it produces rather than prevents or addresses violence, and that shared practices of care and collective self-determination

can better meet our needs than systems based in extraction and domination

Many people fear life without current forms of government because they can't imagine building systems we need to survive "to scale." They worry about the capacity to produce vaccines and our ability to rescue each other or rebuild after fires and storms. But current systems of domination already leave millions without vaccines, disaster preparation, and emergency services. Governments aren't saving us from disaster; they convert each crisis into an opportunity for more wealth concentration. They are ensuring our imminent destruction at a species level. People are *more* capable of collaborating, innovating, demonstrating solidarity, and saving each other without systems like police, military, private property, and borders. People fear that the transition away from current structures will be violent and bloody but fail to recognize that there already is mass suffering, violence, and premature death—and that this is worsening in the face of ecological crisis.

Hundreds of years of government counterinsurgency have ensured, even among abolitionists, widespread ignorance of the histories of anti-state ideas and interventions and caricatures of "anarchy" and "anarchism." Perhaps the most dangerous of these is that anti-state or anarchist ideas are white and patriarchal. In this time of predictable co-optation and reformism, abolitionism must be defined by our actions and responses. It requires us to rigorously engage the question of the state, drawing from anti-colonial, anti-racist and feminist analysis and practices that reimagine infrastructure and care outside of centralized authority and the domination it inevitably requires. Abolitionists already follow anarchist principles of voluntary association, direct action, and mutual aid in efforts to dismantle dominant institutions and build a new world through decentralized experimentation. The more vigorously we can engage this question and take up the wisdom of past and present anti-state resistance formations, the better our chance to build the world we are collectively imagining.

Erica Caines, "Thoughts on Abolition" (2024)

Politics can change and evolve. Considering the dialectical nature of embodied knowledge or "lived experience" and politics, it is imperative to acknowledge that these processes inherently demand change and evolution. In other words, what one strongly believes can be reconsidered and analyzed alongside objective material analysis, as both are theoretically in a constant state of development. Since 2020, there has been a gradual realization about the limitations of various strategies, ideologies, and political approaches, particularly in the context of using "abolition" as a catch-all umbrella.

To grasp the U.S. state in its specific and complex dimensions, one needs to recognize the conditions of colonized people as arising from a "carceral relationship with the state"; within this context, abolition as a political stance appeared to be a natural and fitting response. Despite occasional questions or perceived inconsistencies in certain proclamations, the political principles of abolition seemed valid enough to warrant organizing around. Our engagement with "abolition" manifested through actions such as joining coalitions with abolitionists, initiating a book club to explore unanswered questions, and advocating for the incorporation of abolition frameworks in various organizing efforts.

However, as we delved into a more profound understanding of anti-imperialist and Black internationalist frameworks, particularly through direct involvement with Africans in locations like Cuba or Nicaragua, it became evident that the application of an abolition framework fell short in comprehensively analyzing the interconnected conditions faced by colonized people. Acknowledging our own gradual process of reevaluating abolition, it's clear that certain conclusions wouldn't have been reached without a serious consideration of organizing against the primary contradiction—imperialism. This deliberate focus compels an in-depth exploration of the conditions in the Third World, prompting an examination of the imperialist history and structures responsible for shaping those conditions.

As we delved into a more principled grasp of scientific socialism and gained ideological clarity through study and organizing, the constraints of "abolition" became apparent. Domestically, these limitations are observable in the continual redefinition and individualization of "abolition," adapting ad hoc as needed, influenced by the motivations of those employing it. This term has been embraced by activists and academics alike, resulting in varying connotations within different contexts. This ultimately prompts self-proclaimed abolitionists to assert that "abolition is a practice." In examining this perspective on abolition, a noticeable trend emerges—the reluctance to systematically map out the practice in a principled and scientific manner. Notably, there is a deliberate avoidance of engaging in discussions about socialism and the concept of a socialist state within the framework of abolition.

This raises the question of why abolition, portrayed as a practice, is articulated separately from, or even in lieu of, the endeavor to construct socialism. If the fulfillment of abolition lies in ensuring basic needs are met, it prompts further inquiry into the disproportionate emphasis on mutual aid over mutual comradeship and organizational discipline. Moreover, when viewing the state as a collective entity perpetuating mass incarceration through wielded power, the absence of emphasis on class struggle becomes conspicuous. This leads to a broader reflection on the intricate intersections between abolition, socialism, and the dynamics of power within a society.

Within the rhetoric of abolitionist discourse, often characterized by the envisioning of new societal paradigms (new worlds), there is a notable omission of emphasis on the practical process of 'building towards,' overshadowed by a prevailing idealism. This shift is not occurring in isolation; rather, it unfolds within the broader context of a mounting anti-communist sentiment that impedes a comprehensive linkage between the end goal of abolition and the final stage of communism.

Consequently, there is a noticeable absence of concerted efforts directed at organizing around workers' struggles, encompassing issues such as employment, housing, and education, to establish a foundation for an eventual vanguard capable of securing liberated zones and community control. The current landscape is characterized by localized organizing that responds to immediate concerns rather than strategically preparing for systemic change. This is particularly evident in the negligence of recognizing domestic and global imperialism as interconnected challenges, exemplified by the expanding department of defense budget, which includes federal policing, with minimal organized resistance on a mass scale.

Internationally, the constraints of universal (read: U.S.- centric) abolition frameworks have tangible implications for the progression toward a multipolar world and, crucially, for the self-determination of the masses in those nations. . . . This framework has inadvertently served the interests of the US, which uses "human rights" hypocrisy to encourage its citizens to take positions on nations it is attempting to destabilize to advance its hegemony. Whether it be the constant coverage of protests against policing or finding members of the diaspora to speak out against the "police state," abolition, as a non-concrete framework, has been a useful tool for the U.S.' foreign policy. Here we can see the alignment between anti-state and anti-communist rhetoric becoming synonymous with "abolition."

The widespread adoption of the "All Cops Are Bad" (ACAB) mantra has, to some extent, oversimplified the nuanced considerations surrounding the roles of individuals within the state, blurring distinctions between those contributing to state-building for socialism and those defending the socialist project. The flippant application of "ACAB" poses a risk by oversimplifying the class character of policing, portraying it universally and equating all states, despite their diverse histories, as one and the same. This portrayal, which deems the mere existence of cops as inherently negative, discourages an exploration of the nuanced aspects of this concept. This contradiction is intensifying over time. Simultaneously, the reconsideration of a universal (read: U.S.-centric) abolition framework is ironically labeled as "counter-revolutionary."

While I don't inherently reject the idea of abolition, similar to my stance on decolonization, the evident issue lies in frameworks lacking clear ideologies—they tend to deviate and morph into placeholders, susceptible to individual interpretation. The problem arises when these frameworks become substitutes for personalized meanings, leading to a fragmentation of the concept. This absence of a solid ideological foundation is precisely why there is a lack of a cohesive abolition "movement" and instead an abundance of self-proclaimed abolitionists, each defining and pursuing the concept in their own way.

Where do we go from here?

FACILITATION GUIDE

Week 1 | Who are We? What is Knowledge?

In our first session, we try to do multiple things. We introduce our participants to our guiding principles—abolitionist, internationalist, intersectional, and participatory—and specifically to what these mean for collective study. We get to know one another and develop community norms. We begin to build the collective confidence to study together and to develop ourselves as organic intellectuals. And we begin to understand how that study will impact how we understand the world—and how we work to change it.

Grounding: We need to understand how the world functions in order to dismantle it, and while our personal experiences can shed light on that functioning, *experience is not knowledge*. We take our experiences as a starting point to study how they relate to oppressive systems: capitalism, colonialism, white supremacy, and patriarchy in particular. And we study *together* because the experiences and perspectives that others bring to the table help enrich our understanding of those systems. Our enemies don't want us to study, and much less to study together.

Participatory study is like a stew, and we all bring ingredients to throw in the pot. So let's get cooking! We begin by collecting motivations, perspectives, and experiences, guided by questions like these:

- What motivates you? Why are you here?
- What struggles have you been involved in or thinking about?
- What do you want to understand better?

Then we shift slightly to ask:

- What did you hear from *other* people about why they are here?

Facilitators can begin to develop the practice of pulling some pieces out of what they're hearing and connecting these to the broader goals of participatory education.

Reading: We begin slowly. Since participants haven't read ahead of time, in this session we take turns collectively reading aloud the short passages from Gramsci, Marx, and Bambara. Ask:

- Where does change come from?
- Why does the way we think matter?
- What does Gramsci mean when he says we're all intellectuals?

Note that we will be working with some unfamiliar ideas and seemingly complex concepts during this seminar. Think of these as *tools* to decode and analyze reality, nothing more. If they are useful, *good*, if not, they can be discarded and replaced.

Key Takeaways:

- Gramsci was an Italian communist, and he wrote these passages from a fascist prison in the 1920s after a series of failed communist uprisings across Europe. The question he's trying to answer is why those revolutions failed when the 1917 Russian Revolution seemed to succeed so quickly, with a small number of militants seizing state power. His answer was that in Russia the state was everything, whereas in Europe power was about much more than the state, so when revolutionaries attacked the state, a different *kind* of power revealed itself.

- That power is what he calls *hegemony*—not military power or force, but the power of common sense, of ideas cultivated in civil society institutions. Hegemonic power is therefore about those ways of thinking that uphold and sustain the status quo, but this isn't simply a question of ideas: it's about how those ideas are *institutionalized* and spread by schools, churches, and political parties.
- Think: if we could seize the White House by force today, we still wouldn't have "power," because that power is embedded in how millions of people think and what they believe. And there would be no way to hold onto power without without shifting culture and ideas. What we call *counter-hegemony* therefore means building alternatives to this hegemonic structure. Again, this isn't just about ideas, but about developing new and better arguments to "grip the masses"—in Marx's words—training revolutionary intellectuals and building new counter-institutions—our own parties, organizations, and educational spaces to develop a *new* common sense.
- It is because hegemony matters so much that Gramsci emphasizes the role of intellectuals to either uphold or undermine the status quo. He divides them roughly into two categories.
    - *Traditional* intellectuals justify, explain, and uphold the hegemonic status quo. Think political and religious leaders, media talking heads, and most professors.

    - *Organic* intellectuals build counter-hegemonic ideas for an emerging class, movement, or process of change, and so rather than reflecting the status quo they transform and replace existing ideas. Note that this doesn't mean they are inherently progressive or revolutionary: neoconservatives, radical neoliberals, and fascists, are all fighting a war of ideas to shift our common sense to the right.
- A hegemonic *crisis* is when the existing common sense breaks down and can no longer explain the world in a convincing way, creating radical space (on the left and the right) for alternative explanations.
- In short, *ideas matter*, but they matter most when they gain traction and are spread by material institutions.

Transitioning:

- What is our current hegemonic culture?
- What would counter-hegemonic culture look like, and how do we build it?
- What does a revolutionary abolitionist intellectual *do*?
- Are we in a hegemonic crisis?

Week 2 | What Are We Up Against?

We have seen how our own individual experiences become *knowledge* through the process of collective study. We study the world to understand how repressive carceral structures function, and we study together to collectivize our many experiences and enrich our understanding. In this session, we deepen both pieces by studying materialist analysis and collectively mapping the world we're up against.

Readings: either collectively or in small groups, debrief on Marx's "Theses" and Freire's *Pedagogy* with the following study questions in mind:

- What is a materialist analysis, and is it the opposite of idealism?
- How is the pedagogy of the oppressed materialist?

Key Takeaways:

- Marx is famously a *materialist*, who rejects the *idealism* of prior German philosophers like Hegel and Kant. But this short text from the young Marx begins with a critique of "all hitherto existing materialism" (including Feuerbach). Why? Because *bad* materialism sees the world as an object separate from the humans that make it and "forgets that circumstances are changed by men." As a result, this "contemplative materialism" tends to be abstract and scholastic. And he praises idealism for developing "the active side," even if *bad* idealism is also too abstract and disconnected from reality.
- Against both bad materialism and bad idealism, "revolutionary practice" combines the best elements of both: it sees the world as material, but not out of our reach. We make and remake the material world through human activity. Which is why he famously says, in Thesis 11, that previous philosophers (even materialist ones!) have only interpreted the world whereas "the point is to change it."
- This means that ideas/idealism and reality/materialism are *not* opposed! Too much materialism and the world can't change; too much idealism and we think changing our ideas is all that matters. So Marx is looking for a balance. As we saw in the Marx passage from last week, "theory becomes a material force as soon as

it has gripped the masses," and as we saw for Gramsci, this has *everything* to do with counter-hegemonic education.

- Freire was a revolutionary Brazilian educator who was jailed and later exiled under the dictatorship in the 1960s. He begins from a similar question: if the oppressed are so indoctrinated by their oppressors, how can they free themselves? And he answers that: "the solution cannot be understood in idealistic terms," i.e. education isn't purely about ideas (note that for Marx and Freire, "objective" and "material" usually correspond, as do "subjective" and "ideal"). Instead, education needs to begin with seeing the world, as Marx had argued, as something that can be transformed, starting with "the concrete situation" of oppression. To look at the world *objectively* doesn't mean we can't change it *subjectively*. As for Marx, both are necessary.
- But changing the world (through liberated education) "requires political power and the oppressed have none." So what can we do? Freire identifies two different stages with corresponding strategies. Since in the first stage we don't control what he calls "systematic education," we can and must launch alternative (counter-hegemonic) "educational projects" that challenge, confront, and unmask the existing world to get more people committed to the struggle. It is only in the second stage—marked by radical change—that we can fully replace oppressive "systematic education" with liberated education. And both stages are essential: we begin with small alternatives but we aim for total transformation.
- Again, the main takeaway is that the world is objective and material, but not so much that our ideas don't matter. We build a counter-hegemonic education to change ideas (our subjective understanding), but more importantly to build a revolutionary movement that will transform the objective structure of the system.

Activity: break into groups with markers and paper for a 15-minute collective mapping activity guided by the following questions:

- What are we up against? What systems do we confront every day in our lives and in our organizing? How do these relate to each other? Where do they come from?
- Map out the constellation of how these structures relate to each other.
- Finish with a 5-minute rotating gallery walk to observe and contribute further connections to what other groups have mapped out.
- Reconvene for reportbacks on how the systems we have all identified relate functionally to each other.

Transition: as we have seen in our mapping activity, we confront several interlocking systems, but capitalism is key. Ask:

- How does capitalism impact our lives?
- What would a class analysis of your city tell us?
- What would it *fail* to tell us?

Collect some responses for discussion before introducing some basic Marxist concepts, specifically: means of production, relations of production, and modes of production; capitalism as our overarching mode of production; and the centrality of surplus-value, profit, and exploitation under capitalism.

Week 3 | The History of Class Struggle

Last week, we collectively mapped out the repressive, exploitative, and carceral structures that we're up against, how they connect and relate to one another, and we began to analyze capitalism in particular. In this session, we recap and strengthen our understanding of some basic concepts—materialism vs. idealism, and modes, means, and relations of production—before mapping these onto a broad view of historical change that we will complicate in the weeks to come.

Readings: turn to some neighbors and spend 5–7 minutes discussing the excerpts from *The Communist Manifesto* with the following questions in mind:

- What does it mean to say that history is defined by class struggle?
- We live under capitalism—how did we get here?
- What is the bourgeoisie? What is the proletariat?

Key Takeaways:

- There are different ways to think about historical change. We could assume that things are always improving and that change comes slowly over time. Or we could see historical change as the product of *struggle*. The basic word for this view is *dialectics*, but don't get distracted when you hear it: just think conflict and struggle. Now, we have talked about idealism vs, materialism, and about the need for both pieces. Dialectics can be either: a clash of ideas and visions, a clash of material forces in the world, or a combination of the two.
- While ideas are crucial, Marx and Engels see history as moving through
    - material development of the forces of production (society's ability to produce the things we need), and
    - political struggle or revolution, which marks the transition between overarching modes of production.
- Roughly speaking, these modes are:

- "Primitive" communism: ask someone to read aloud the first sentence of the *Manifesto*, then read the footnote. It isn't true that *all* societies are divided by class: early communal societies were not, in part because the low level of the forces of production prevented the production of *surplus*.
- Slavery, divided into master (exploiter) and slave (exploited), which becomes possible in human history when surplus is produced.
- Feudalism, divided into feudal lord (exploiter) and serf (exploited)
- Capitalism, divided into bourgeoisie (exploiter) and proletariat (exploited)
- Explain the transition between these: development of the forces of production create tensions, and class struggle by the exploited unleashes revolutions. Example: the 1789 French Revolution is often seen as the moment that the bourgeoisie overthrew the feudal order before then using the state to fully install a capitalist system.

Transitioning:

- Ask: Why do Marx and Engels describe capitalism and the bourgeoisie as "revolutionary"? This seems strange, but it isn't a compliment, it's a technical statement about how they constantly revolutionize the forces of production. Why? *Competition*. The need to compete for profit speeds up our ability to produce things like never before. This becomes crucial (and problematic) when we try to understand the difference between "primitive" and future communism on a global level. Whereas early communal societies required members to work constantly just to survive, future communism would use the forces of production developed under capitalism to work *less*, not more.

- Ask: what problems do you see with this view of history?

Activity: Lineages of Class Analysis. We're talking about materialist and class analysis, and starting from some basic Marxist categories. But class is all around us, and class struggle includes many movements that don't even identify as Marxist. Break into 2–4 groups to collectively read *either* the Black Panther Party Program or the Combahee River Collective statement. Ask yourselves and one another:

- What means of production are addressed in the document? Modes of production?
- How do relations of production explain Black liberation, and Black feminism in particular?
- What does abolition look like in these statements?

Regroup to summarize and report back, share passages that resonate, and reflect on the shifts you can see between the two documents published a decade apart.

Week 4 | Where Do Slavery & Colonialism Fit?

So far, we have learned some basic Marxist concepts and mapped these onto a rough outline of how history changes through class struggle (i.e. dialectically). While this framework is useful, it needs to be fleshed out more fully, by asking what Marxist categories help us to understand versus what they obscure. In particular, we ask how *other* oppressive structures that we have discussed—particularly slavery, colonialism, and patriarchy—fit in this framework? One key concept that we use as leverage to answer this question is *primitive accumulation.*

Readings: either collectively or in small groups, spend 5–7 minutes breaking down and discussing the Marx and Luxemburg readings with an eye to the questions:

- What is so-called primitive accumulation?
- What is the role of slavery and colonialism within capitalism?

Key Takeaways:

- In the *Manifesto*, Marx and Engels had already mentioned colonialism and slavery as foundations for the initial expansion of capitalism, and this later passage from *Capital* expands on that idea. There was *nothing* natural about the emergence of capitalism, and it didn't emerge through the gradual expansion of the "free market"—a libertarian myth and contradiction in terms. Instead, it was the product of extreme *violence* and *state intervention* that helped launch and generalize capitalism as an overarching mode of production.
- Marx calls this violent intervention "primitive" (or "original") accumulation, by which he means that it took place at the earliest stages of capitalism. For Marx, primitive accumulation took two broad forms:
    - *In Europe,* it created the working class (or proletariat) through a process of dispossession. The "great enclosures" expelled peasants from previously communal lands, stripping them of access to the means of production (or means of survival). Unable to provide for themselves, they were forced to work for others. This wasn't enough to force them

into factories, however, and so the government needed to criminalize poverty, vagrancy, and vagabondage, brutally deploying the police to punish those who refused to work. It was only over time that people slowly forgot their memories of pre-capitalist ways of life and passively accepted wage labor.

    - *In the colonies*, it created capitalists overnight through a massive infusion of wealth derived from colonization and slavery. Rather than a slow process of accumulating and reinvesting profits, capitalists "sprang up like mushrooms overnight" through state funding, contracts, and the hyper exploitation of colonized and enslaved people, *launching* capitalism into existence globally. As Marx writes, "the veiled slavery of the wage workers in Europe needed, for its pedestal, slavery pure and simple in the new world."

- Rosa Luxemburg, writing fifty years later, was one of the first to emphasize the ways that so-called primitive accumulation *never ended*. In part, this is because she saw these same dynamics that had emerged within Europe (breaking up communal structures, creating proletarians, and moreover seeking markets for capitalist goods) happening on *both* sides of the colonial divide. Collective self-sufficiency is the enemy of profit, so capitalism needs to destroy all "natural economies" to create space for itself and workers to exploit. "Each new colonial expansion," she writes, "is accompanied . . . by a relentless battle of capital against the social and economic ties of the natives, who are also forcibly robbed of their means of production and labor power." Where Marx saw this as an early stage of capitalism, with violence eventually being replaced by capitalism's "automatic" functions, Luxemburg shows how capitalism's existence requires permanent and ongoing violence.

- We see this ongoing process all around us, and in the other texts for this week. Angela Davis shows the role of women as the glue holding together the community of slaves as a structure of self-preservation and resistance—what we might call "reproductive labor" in its broadest sense. Attacks on enslaved women—and sexual violence in particular—she sees as counterinsurgent campaigns against the community of resistance. Other thinkers and organizations, like the Red Nation, identify violence against Indigenous women—bearers of community—as playing a similar role in capitalist expansion. Finally, Robin D.G. Kelley describes the findings of the Ferguson Commission as an explicit example of primitive accumulation in the present: "Summons and warrants are used as a kind of racial tax, an extraction of surplus directly by the state without producing anything besides discipline and terror and the reproduction of the state; in a word, revenue by primitive accumulation."

Activity: Primitive Accumulation Today. Put the definition of primitive accumulation up on the screen and take 15 minutes in breakout groups with paper and markers to collectively map out the ways that primitive accumulation is a continuous and ongoing process. What does it look like in the world and your city? Collect reflections and share.

Week 5 | Many Paths to Socialism

Last week, we complicated the basic Marxist view of history with an understanding of primitive accumulation as an ongoing and uneven process that points toward different paths not only to capitalism, but to socialism and communism as well. This week expands on this unevenness by centering colonialism and asking what it means to think of capitalism as a hierarchical global system based not only on economic exploitation but also on colonial dispossession, extraction, and racial hierarchy.

Activity: What is colonialism and what does it do? Break into four groups for 15 minutes to collectively map out the local and global effects of colonial expansion and the capitalist domination it brought.

- Give each group markers and pre-drawn maps, numbered 1–4, of the Atlantic circuit showing at least Europe, Africa, North and South America.
- Prompt with some key dates. Some that we use include: 1440 (early European colonialism and enslavement of Africans), 1487 (rounding of the Cape of Good Hope), 1492 (of course), 1521 (the fall of Tenochtitlan), 1551 (Spanish debates on humanity of Indigenous people), 1619/1620 (slavery and colonization in North America), 1676 (Bacon's rebellion), 1789 (the French Revolution), 1791–1804 (the Haitian Revolution), add your own!
- Ask each group to use those dates and others to mark crucial moments of connection, movement, and conflict guided by the question. Draw arrows connecting different regions to illustrate colonial dynamics and report back to the larger group.

Readings: We talked about how slavery and colonialism are crucial not only for launching capitalism as a global system, but how they play an ongoing role in sustaining it as well. This radically complicates Marx's view of history, as he would eventually come to realize.

Key Takeaways:

- One key place we can see this is in his 1881 correspondence with the militant Russian socialist Vera Zasulich. Zasulich has read

Capital, with its description of how communist revolution will emerge from the most highly developed capitalist countries. This definitely isn't Russia, which is still mostly feudal, but which also has traditional communal structures in the countryside.

- Zasulich's question is this: what do socialists do under these circumstances? Do they sit around waiting decades or centuries for capitalism to develop, destroying communal society in the process? Or can we use those existing communal structures to *build socialism directly*? Her questions push Marx to reconsider his linear view of history and admit that there can be different paths to socialism and that so-called primitive communism could provide a basis for these alternatives.
- Why does this historical debate matter? Because *most of the world* confronts a question similar to the one Zasulich posed, making the question of how to proceed toward socialism without passing through capitalism central for many Third World Marxists. The key difference between communism of the past and the future, recall, is the level of development of the forces of production, but since capitalism has *already* played its role in amplifying our technological and productive capacities, it should be theoretically possible to infuse exiting pre-capitalist communal structures with that new technological capacity. This is no easy task, however.
- Two Third World Marxists who confronted similar scenarios were José Carlos Mariátegui in Peru and Walter Rodney in Guyana. When Mariátegui surveyed "Peruvian reality" in the 1920s, what he saw was radically different from European capitalism. Peru was mostly feudal, with some remnants of slavery, very little capitalism, and an Indigenous collective economy that had survived the near-extermination of the Incan empire. Mariátegui argues that rather than helping to build capitalism on the path toward communism, Peruvian socialists should tap into existing

communal structures to build "Indo-American socialism." And he points toward the concept of economic "dependency" as a way of understanding that the global system doesn't want capitalist development in the Third World—it just wants labor, land, and natural resources.

- Writing in the 1970s, Rodney analyzes colonialism, slavery, and underdevelopment in both Africa and his native Guyana (a former British colony in South America). He argues that countries aren't simply "developed" or "underdeveloped," but that under/development is a *relation* through which some (European, colonial countries) develop by actively *underdeveloping* others. Like Mariátegui, he argues that Africa didn't undergo the same progression of modes of production and class formations that Marx had seen in Europe. Instead, like much of Latin America, it saw a combination of feudal and collective socialist structures alongside small pockets of capitalism. One key difference, however, is that while slavery was implanted in the Western Hemisphere, Africa—the *source* of enslaved labor—did not itself see a mode of production based on slavery. Rodney offers us a key concept for grasping these different realities and their implications for liberation struggles: *uneven development*.

<u>Transitioning</u>: groups return to their maps in a rotating gallery walk, spending 5–7 minutes addressing the *local* impact of colonialism, in Europe (Map 1), Africa (Map 2), British North America (Map 3), and Latin America (Map 4). Add observations and then rotate before collective share-out. Some key questions posed by all this include:

- How does seeing capitalism as a global system reshape how we understand resistance?

- How does future communism relate to "primitive" collectivism and Indigenous structures?

Week 6 | Black Reconstruction, Part I

We've been studying colonialism as the expansion of capitalism to the global scale through violence and ongoing primitive accumulation, including the theft of land and forced labor. Modern slavery is born out of this process, and even though it takes a slightly different *form* in the US, we shouldn't fall into the common idea that colonialism and slavery are completely distinct and separable systems, or that our struggles shouldn't be anchored in a shared history. So as we dive into *Black Reconstruction*, it's important to remember that we're still talking about these long colonial legacies.

Reading: Du Bois wrote *Black Reconstruction* in 1935 to set the record straight on the meaning of Reconstruction, the decade following the end of the Civil War that had been severely discredited by later historians, who argued that it was a wasteful failure, a disaster, and that in short, Black people weren't capable of self-government. In the course of making this argument, however, Du Bois rewrites the whole history of the Civil War, its meaning and outcome, and the role of Black people, enslaved and later free, in determining the meaning of that history.

Activity: Breakout into four groups for 10 minutes, with each group responding to one of the four study questions below. Report back in order, 1–4, with facilitators adding context and connection.

Key Takeaways:

- Why does Du Bois speak of "The Black Worker" and "The White Worker"? At this point in his life, Du Bois is increasingly Marxist, more concerned with economic categories and class struggle than with appealing to the moral conscience of (white) America. However, as we have already seen, many Marxists held to a very rigid view of history in which slavery belonged to the past and class struggle meant factory workers. Du Bois is disrupting those definitions and that history by arguing that *slavery was an essential part of capitalism,* not a prior historical stage (as theorists of "Racial Capitalism" insist today). As a result, enslaved people were *workers,* and moreover strategically central to the capitalist economy (and the struggle against it). Du Bois speaks of the *white* worker in part to underline the contradictions that separate black from white workers, but also the possibility of a revolutionary alliance between the two.

- Why does he speak of "the general strike" and what does he mean by this? Like the category of "worker," the general strike is traditionally reserved for industrial workers in the capitalist core. Du Bois rejects this, showing how at the outset of the Civil War, enslaved black workers watched and waited to be certain where their interests lay before walking off the job en masse (some five hundred thousand). This mattered because while white workers in the South were fighting the war, black workers were growing the food, so the black general strike crippled the Southern war effort. While Marxists often see general strikes as highly organized and coordinated, moreover, Du Bois is describing something more spontaneous and which couldn't have been organized—but which was hugely impactful nonetheless.
- Was the Civil War about slavery, yes or no? This is the question! And the answer begins with a yes *and* a no. On the "no" side: neither side wanted to free the slaves. Lincoln was *not* an abolitionist: he wanted to preserve the Union with or without slavery, and even sought to ship all black people off to colonies elsewhere.

The South *was* explicitly fighting for slavery, and for the political power of the slave states in Congress, which provoked secession. That power had been overstated by the Three-Fifths Compromise, which *over*represented planters by allowing them to count enslaved people for congressional representation. But here's the key: even though the Civil War wasn't initially a war to end slavery, both the general strike and then black soldiers joining the war effort, *made* it about abolition. Lincoln issued the Emancipation Proclamation because he needed black soldiers, and because making the war about slavery would prevent England and France from recognizing the Confederacy.

- Who freed the slaves? Who won the Civil War? Enslaved people *freed themselves,* and in so doing were ultimately the ones who determined the outcome and the meaning of the war. They made it a war against slavery because they were the only ones with the strategic power to win it, withdrawing their labor from the South and bestowing it on the North, first as workers, then as scouts and spies, and finally as soldiers. The South couldn't arm them, but the North (after much debate) realized it *had* to. Du Bois notes that fighting for freedom and killing white men to save the Union was what ultimately convinced many that black people were truly human. The "price of the disaster of war," however, was not just freedom (the Thirteenth Amendment), but also the demand for equal citizenship (the Fourteenth Amendment) and ultimately the vote as well (the Fifteenth Amendment).

Week 7 | Black Reconstruction, Part II

This week covers the second half of *Black Reconstruction,* dealing roughly with what comes *after* the war—the fight for black citizenship and the right to vote—but also about what else was needed to maintain freedom. It deals with the brief moment in which "the slave went free; stood a brief moment in the sun; then moved back again toward slavery." In other words, Du Bois shows that Reconstruction was an unprecedented moment of possibility and the high point of American democracy, and how its volent destruction set us back a century and explains much of where we are today.

Activity: Breakout into 4 groups for 10 minutes, with each group responding to one of the four study questions. Report back in order, 1–4, with facilitators adding context and connection.

Key Takeaways:

- Who benefited from Reconstruction? *Everyone*. Reconstruction, especially as we saw in black-majority South Carolina, improved the lives of everyone: women, children, and poor whites who had been excluded from politics by literacy tests and property requirements and subject to debt prisons all benefited. Recall that Du Bois had called the black worker the "ultimate exploited," a reference to Marx's universal class (the proletariat) who can only free themselves by freeing *everyone*, and Reconstruction shows this to have been true (with the major exception of Indigenous people).
- How and why did Reconstruction end? Concretely, it ended with the contested 1877 election, which put Hayes in power in exchange for withdrawing federal troops from the South. But why did this happen on a deeper, structural level? Because northern capitalists had supported abolition and even the black vote, but only as long as it benefited them in their competition with southern planters. Without federal troops as the *force* upholding the political right to vote, the KKK and other white terror groups stepped in to prevent black people from voting and roll back their political power. For Du Bois, it is a world-historic tragedy that the

KKK (and later the police) were drawn from the very same poor whites who had benefited from Reconstruction.

- What were the international consequences of Reconstruction's defeat? For Du Bois, the US became "a reactionary force" globally. Meaning that the domination and exploitation of labor and enforced white supremacy at home became a framework for US imperial expansion, which truly begins just a few decades later with the so-called Spanish-American War in 1898—and the seizure of Cuba, Puerto Rico, the Philippines, and Guam. There's a *direct* connection between domestic and international white supremacy, against which Du Bois speaks of a global "dark proletariat" of exploited Third World workers as the basis for revolutionary change.
- What did Du Bois mean by saying formerly enslaved people moved "back toward slavery"? The defeat of Reconstruction meant not only rolling back *political* rights but also *economic* reconstruction. There was no economic reform, no distribution of land, no forty acres and a mule. Formerly enslaved people were still poor, with no access to the means of production, and so had no alternative to sharecropping and eventually debt prisons, alongside many poor whites. Black Codes were a repeat of early primitive accumulation, particularly vagrancy laws that made it illegal to be homeless and jobless. Once in jail, they were subjected to the forced labor of convict leasing, in line with the loophole in the Thirteenth Amendment that allows the enslavement of convicts even today. Some found themselves re-enslaved on the *same* plantations they had been "freed" from only years before. The defeat of Reconstruction paved the way for a series of new institutions that emerged to continue to provide the same economic and racial control that that slavery had.

Transitioning: Collectively or in small groups, brainstorm and discuss the legacies of Reconstruction's defeat for the present, guided by these questions:

- Where can we see ongoing legacies of colonialism and the failure of Reconstruction in our everyday lives—nationally, regionally, and locally?
- Think in terms of:
    - space: segregation, containment, exclusion, displacement
    - economics: intergenerational wealth inequalities, unemployment
    - politics: voting rights, gerrymandering, and disenfranchisement
    - education, safety, violence, housing
    - carceral systems like policing and prisons

Week 8 | Philadelphia: Crucible of Abolition

Our work is based in Philadelphia, both because that's where we live and work, but also because Philadelphia plays an outsized role in abolitionist struggles past and present. Those located elsewhere can approach this week in several different ways: you can read and study elements of Philadelphia abolitionist history as we have done, you can replace this segment with your own local histories and resources, or you can combine the two. In any case, it's worth beginning from the failures of Reconstruction and what this meant for the place and the people in question.

Readings: While we considered many possible sources for this week, we found that movement elder and comrade Mumia Abu-Jamal did an amazing job of synthesizing both historical moments and the broader political terrain across the city.

Key Takeaways:

- For Mumia, following Frederick Douglass, Philadelphia's location has everything to do with its central role in abolitionist movements and how race continues to operate in the city today. Technically in the North, it was and remains a very southern city in many senses.
- But paradoxically, being part of a "free" state meant that the mechanisms of economic exploitation, discrimination, and segregation were developed much earlier than in the Jim Crow South—not to mention white mob violence. Poor white ethnic communities, Italian and Irish in particular, struggled against one another, and both against black Philadelphians, for political power.
- The crowning achievement of this process of white incorporation, much like the cross-class alliance of the southern Klan, came with the political rise of Frank Rizzo, first as police commissioner and later as mayor. It was Rizzo himself who provided the political backdrop for Mumia's own experience with the Philadelphia chapter of the Black Panther Party.
- Against this openly racist power structure, however, Philadelphia was also an early example of "black faces in high places," or the politics of representation. The city had black police as early as the 1890s, and the black leadership class would take over power after Rizzo's departure, only to drop a murderous bomb on the MOVE Organization, of which Mumia was a member, in 1985.

Activity: either in class or as a project, collectively assemble a local abolitionist timeline that brings together key moments of struggle, movements and organizations in your city across the centuries. Think particularly in terms of:

- economic structure and class exploitation
- racial dynamics and carceral institutions
- localized struggles against slavery and for freedom and equality
- local organizations and the struggles they led

Many of these histories are untold, and their importance is underestimated. Building a bridge to the past is also building a bridge toward the future. Ours is hosted on Miro: https://miro.com/app/board/o9J_lhuR_BU=/.

Week 9 | Decolonization & Third World Revolution

Our curriculum anchors abolition and reconstruction not only in the institution of chattel slavery, but within broader histories of colonial domination and anticolonial resistance. This week returns to this thread by providing a brief overview of the anticolonial wave of the mid-twentieth century before turning to the readings for insight. Given the political moment this project was born in, we take this week as an opportunity to test our abolitionist and decolonial lenses by applying them to the contemporary struggle for Palestinian liberation.

Activity: We begin from the striking parallels between two poems about death and resistance against all odds written more than a century apart by black communist Claude McKay and Palestinian poet Refaat Alareer. Invite participants to read the poems aloud, listen to existing audio versions, or engage in a comparative analysis of both.

Readings: Our readings for this week bring together three revolutionary manifestos from very different times and places, but which share an underlying emphasis on colonial domination and anticolonial resistance.

Key Takeaways:

- Fanon's *Wretched of the Earth* is widely seen as a "bible" of decolonization, particularly for its unflinching analysis of both colonial violence and its anticolonial counterpart—to which many turned in the aftermath of the Palestinian resistance offensive of October 7th. Fanon was a Black man born in the French colony of Martinique, making him uniquely positioned to analyze *both* racism (in *Black Skin, White Masks*) and colonialism (in *Wretched*)—and the interconnections of both.
- A trained psychiatrist, Fanon was stationed in a French clinic in colonial Algeria in the mid-1950s, where he would treat both French and Algerian patients—seeking to repair the psychological damage of torture on both its perpetrators and victims. In 1956, he realized that it was impossible to heal individuals when the world itself was sick—a theory he calls "sociogeny"—and resigned to join the Algerian Revolution. He dictated *Wretched* on his deathbed, dying at 36 just before the revolution succeeded.
- For Fanon, colonialism is violence in its purest form, and decolonization is also violent for three interlocking reasons:
    1. Because the colonizer won't leave voluntarily;
    2. Because the colonized needs to struggle in order to regain individual and collective self-confidence, and to eliminate the inferiority complex that colonialism implants in the colonized (although this could in theory involve combative tactics that don't involve physical violence);

3. Because *anything* the colonized does is seen as violent regardless (think of how the victims of police murder are turned into aggressors, or how nonviolent tactics of Palestinian resistance like BDS or the Great March of Return are criminalized and repressed).

Taken together, these three pieces make it difficult for Fanon to contemplate a truly nonviolent struggle against colonialism. But violence is only the first step, and while decolonization seeks first to get rid of the colonizer, it must ultimately shift toward a project for social transformation to avoid simply falling back into neo-colonialism.

- Decolonization is a long and unfinished struggle that was not completed with the seizure of Third World states in the mid-twentieth century. Mexico's Zapatista rebels make clear just how long this struggle is with their emblematic declaration that "we are the product of 500 years of struggle," i.e. a struggle that began in 1492.
- Some background: the Zapatista army organized in secret for more than a decade in the southern state of Chiapas before rising up publicly on January 1st, 1994—the same day that NAFTA (the North American Free Trade Agreement) came into effect. Two major implications of the agreement were:
  1. it abolished constitutional protections for collective communal lands known as *ejidos*, much like the great enclosures of primitive accumulation;
  2. it opened the Mexican market up to cheap GMO corn from the US.

  NAFTA destroyed the way of life of hundreds of thousands of mostly Indigenous Mexicans, sending many migrating north toward a newly militarized border.
- Encourage students to read the Zapatistas' demands for "work, land, housing, food, healthcare, education, independence,

freedom, democracy, justice, and peace" alongside the strikingly similar list contained in the Black Panther Ten-Point Program

- Finally, the Red Nation's *Red Deal* gives us a contemporary example of what decolonization means today, particularly in the face of climate catastrophe. For the Red Nation, "it's decolonization or extinction," and Indigenous governance is the only possible solution to the challenges we collectively face. But much like Du Bois' analysis of Reconstruction—another unfinished project—decolonization is a universal project *for everyone* that spans the abolition of prisons, police, US imperialism, and borders, and means embracing Indigenous modes of governance, building a caretaking economy, and transforming our relationship to the land and to each other.

Activity: Gaza Breaks Out. As Mariam Barghouti put it, "On October 7th, Gaza Broke Out of Prison." Either collectively or in small groups, use categories from settler colonialism and abolition to decolonization and violence to analyze:

a. Israeli settler colonialism
b. October 7th

What does it mean to take Palestinian liberation seriously as an abolitionist and anticolonial struggle?

Week 10 | What is the State? What is Revolution?

All revolutionaries inevitably confront the question of the state, and this is especially true for those of us who seek to abolish carceral state structures in all their forms. These questions are even more complex for internationalists, for whom the state performs distinct and contradictory functions on the global level. While we don't seek to answer these questions fully for our students, our goal should be to illustrate the stakes of the question and encourage students to take the question of state power seriously.

Reading: much as we did with Marx, we begin with what is often understood as *the* central text on the state in the revolutionary tradition—Lenin's *State and Revolution*—before complicating the picture with the perspective of the revolutionary Third World.

Key Takeaways:

- Lenin writes much of *State and Revolution* between the February and October revolutions of 1917, while a liberal caretaker government attempted to manage what turned out to be unmanageable contradictions between a surging grassroots movement and old ruling elites. The Bolsheviks would eventually break this standoff by seizing state power, which is why Lenin is thinking hard in this interim about what the state means and how it functions to manage otherwise irreconcilable class antagonisms. He starts from the fact that the state *only* emerges in class society, as "an organ for the oppression of one class by the other." So as a very basic starting point, we could say that any true revolution *must* abolish the state, and that a truly egalitarian society would have no need for a state.
- The question is: how do we get there? Here, Lenin is arguing against two different groups: on the one hand, "opportunists" who want to seize the state and use it for their own ends, and on the other, "anarchists" who want to abolish the state immediately. While Marx and Engels had spoken of the "withering away of the state," this can only happen once society has already been radically

transformed. What is the weapon and tool that helps get us there? For Lenin, it's what he calls the *dictatorship of the proletariat*.

- In other words, Lenin foresees a two-step process: the workers seize power and thereby "abolish" the bourgeois state, replacing it with a temporary semi-state under proletarian control, which is used to suppress the capitalists and collectivize the economy. It is only *after* the economy has been reshaped that the "state in general" can gradually "wither away." Note: there's a striking parallel here between the withering away of the state and how abolitionists describe the process of making police and prisons "obsolete." In both cases, repressive institutions can only fully disappear once society has been radically transformed such that they are no longer needed.
- As usual Rodney helps complicate any assumptions we might have about "the" state or its universal function. He has already shown us how so-called historical "stages" of capitalist development in reality exist *unevenly* across the globe. Since state formation is part of this same process, it follows that political forms also emerge unevenly. Since the state emerges to manage class oppression, it follows that the communal societies that Rodney (and Mariátegui) identified as persistent presences in the Global South are also in some sense and some cases, *stateless* societies. Just as these represent a jumping-off point for future communism on the economic level (collective ownership) they could also be seen to model future communism politically (the absence of the state). Not all states are the same, and nor do they perform the same function within the global capitalist system

Activity: Captive Maternals and the state. Collectively or in small groups, take 5–7 minutes to read aloud the passages from Joy

James on the concept of the Captive Maternal, asking the following questions:

- What is the Captive Maternal, and what is its relation to the state?
- In a moment marked by the conscription of black women into imperial power, what alternative does the Captive Maternal offer?
- How does the Captive Maternal complicate Lenin's approach to the state?

Transitioning: our conversation about the state and abolition included a discussion of the rich tradition of Black anarchist theory and practice. Our conversation included militant thinkers like Lucy Parsons, Kuwasi Balagoon, and Lorenzo Kom'boa Ervin, and was guided by the following questions:

- Do Black people, or Black Americans in particular, have a specific relationship to anarchism and the state?
- Is this relationship the same, similar, or different from other Third World and colonized people?
- What resources does Black anarchism offer for navigating complex questions of internationalism and liberation?

Week 11 | Policing & Prisons

When we think about abolition, we tend to think primarily of carceral institutions like police and prisons. Our curriculum circles back to these institutions both because they are crucial for understanding revolutionary abolitionism, but also because they must be understood within a longer history and broader context. We are not *only* against police and prisons: we're against the systems—capitalism, colonialism, white supremacy, and patriarchy—that they represent and uphold. In this session, we *return* to policing and prisons with a broader understanding and sharper analysis.

Grounding: either collectively read aloud or listen to recorded audio of June Jordan's "Poem about Police Violence." Take a moment to quietly reflect on how little has changed.

Reading: our readings for this week provide both an overview of the historical function of policing and prisons, alongside Assata's first-hand account of the specificity of women's experiences in prison.

Key Takeaways:

- *A World Without Police* argues that policing in the US has always been about protecting two basic things: whiteness and property. Police in the South emerged from slave patrols because black people were suddenly "free" and so their movement had to be controlled to assuage white fear, and because plantation owners wanted to ensure a cheap and profitable labor force. Police were originally drawn from the ranks of poor whites—the same constituency and function as the Klan—and compensated by the psychological and material wages of whiteness. While police in the North were often based on the London model of policing, this model was deeply racial and colonial, developing out of the British occupation of Ireland. But if police are synonymous with white capitalist power, the *pig majority* has conscripted a far broader group that included black and brown cops, politicians, judges, prosecutors, and others.
- In *Are Prisons Obsolete?*, Angela Davis provides a history of the prison along similar lines, showing how prisons—like police—emerged as a replacement for slavery after abolition. Not only was the penitentiary a new institution in the eighteenth century, but

it was also seen as a progressive reform: time became the punishment rather than physical violence. Even then, prisons were largely for white men, since black people were enslaved and white women lacked legal standing. This changed after abolition and the transition toward convict leasing, which provided labor discipline without the need to pay black workers a wage—prisons became institutions of racial control.

- Prisoners have always been profitable sources for primitive accumulation and labor extraction, but this increased dramatically with the mass incarceration of the 1980s, and the expansion of privatization, corporate investment, and prison labor. Remember, though, as Ruth Wilson Gilmore often points out, prisons were never *only* about labor—they were also about racial control. And the "prison-industrial complex" should be understood as describing a far broader process in which prison construction served as a redevelopment plan for rural white America.
- Assata Shakur wrote "Women in Prison" a year before her escape to Cuba, aided by Balagoon and others. In it, she provides a detailed account of conditions at Rikers, for women in particular, many of whom were survivors of cycles of abuse both within and outside the system. She documents the power dynamics and psychological superiority enjoyed by guards drawn from the working class, the complexities of intimate relations, and the unspoken fluidity of gender roleplay. And she emphasizes the fact that life in prison isn't all that different from life in communities subject to the same oppressive forces. "Women can never be free in a country that is not free," she writes, and while capitalist exploitation has destroyed community self-sufficiency—and the leading role of generations of black women—she holds out the possibility for a new militant movement to reclaim both.

Activity: break into four groups for 10 minutes, with each group working separately to answer one of this week's study questions, before sharing back with the collective.

Week 12 | Abolition & Reconstruction Today

In our last session, we circle back to where we began by asking what abolition and reconstruction *mean*. But this is less a circle than a spiral, since we have learned so much in the course of twelve weeks that our understanding of these ideas has changed dramatically. We conclude our seminar with a collective conversation about what it would look like to fulfill the unfinished reconstruction project today.

Grounding: return collectively to where we began with a collective conversation guided by the following questions:

- What does abolition mean today?
- What would a reconstructed city look like?
- What kinds of organizations and campaigns already exist that point us in that direction?

Readings: This week has our most contemporary and concrete set of readings, from three organizers: Mariame Kaba, Dean Spade, and Erica Caines. All three challenge us to walk the fine line between reformist accommodation with the system and an all-or-nothing approach which denounces anything less than total and immediate abolition.

Key Takeaways:

- Kaba offers a useful distinction between those "reformist reforms" that serve to uphold policing and potentially abolitionist reforms that could point in more radical directions. While most police reform proposals *increase* both police budgets and contact with oppressed communities, Kaba argues that the only reforms worth supporting *reduce* police budget and contact, and which in general undermine the power of policing as an institution.
- Spade makes a strong case for the idea, already posed in Week 10, that abolition entails the ultimate abolition of the state. Viewing the state not as a protective distributor of resources, but as a parasitic institution that dictates *how much* exploitation, resource extraction, and environmental degradation is acceptable, Spade insists that while we must in fact engage in campaigns that demand resources from the state (like defunding), our ultimate horizon is anti-state.
- Finally, Caines summarizes some contemporary concerns about abolition as a framework that *any* revolutionary abolitionist needs to take seriously. Whereas our contemporary moment has seen both abolition and decolonization watered down, co-opted, and emptied of their most radical content, Caines insists that any truly revolutionary approach must remain connected to global questions of colonial domination and anti-imperialist struggle, and must be anchored in socialist campaigns for working-class power and liberation.

Activity: Pod-Mapping. Break into four groups for 15 minutes for a closing activity guided by the following questions:

- What resources exist in your community, and what resources are lacking?
- How can we gather and share existing community resources while struggling for the things we need.

There are different ways to do this. On the one hand, we distributed individual worksheets for participants to identify resources shared by their own "pod" of family, neighbors, and friends, before then expanding outward in concentric circles toward broader networks, neighborhoods, and communities, and toward those resources we may know about but haven't engaged with yet. Key questions to consider include:

- Who is in your community? What is it made up of?
- What role do you play in your community?
- What are skills you have that you share or would like to share with others?

Thinking larger, we then shifted into a gallery walk, with sheets of paper labeled West Philly, North Philly, South Philly, and Center City. Participants were asked to add to a collective mapping of neighborhood resources, precious places, and community centers in different areas, while those unfamiliar with the areas or resources take note of what is available.

Transitioning:

- What does the next year have in store for the struggle to abolish & rebuild?
- What will *your* roles be in the struggles to come?

BIBLIOGRAPHY

This reader compiles excerpts of texts from the following sources, listed in the order they appear. Many are available online (at the URLs indicated), but not all. We encourage finding the full print editions of the books included in this anthology at the publisher's website and consider supporting these publishers by purchasing their titles for your own library. We thank Common Notions, Seven Stories, Verso, *Spectre Journal, Truthout,* and Hood Communist for their invaluable work in publishing essential abolitionist writings.

Antonio Gramsci, *Selections from the Prison Notebooks* (New York: International Publishers, 1971), Chapter I.1., 5–7, 9, 12.

Karl Marx, "A Contribution To The Critique Of Hegel's Philosophy Of Right," in *Deutsch-Französische Jahrbücher*, 7 & 10 February 1844 in Paris, available at Marxist Internet Archive, https://www.marxists.org/archive/marx/works/1844/df-jahrbucher/law-abs.htm

Toni Cade Bambara, *Deep Sightings & Rescue Missions* (New York: Knopf, 2009), 273–274.

Karl Marx, "Theses on Feuerbach" (1845), *Marx/Engels Selected Works, Volume One*, Progress Publishers, Moscow, USSR, 1969,

13–15, available at Marxist Internet Archive, https://www.marxists.org/archive/marx/works/1845/theses/theses.htm

Paulo Freire, *Pedagogy of the Oppressed* (New York: Continuum, 2000), 48–49, 50–51, 54–55.

Karl Marx and Friedrich Engels, *Manifesto of the Communist Party* (1848), Chapter 1, *Marx/Engels Selected Works, Vol. One*, Progress Publishers, Moscow, 1969, pp. 98–137; available at Marxist Internet Archive, https://www.marxists.org/archive/marx/works/1848/communist-manifesto/.

Black Panther Ten Point Program (October 15,1966), available at Marxist Internet Archive, https://www.marxists.org/history/usa/workers/black-panthers/1966/10/15.htm

The Combahee River Collective Statement (April 1977), In Zillah Eisenstein, ed., *Capitalist Patriarchy and the Case for Socialist Feminism* (Monthly Review Press, 1979), 362–72.

Karl Marx, *Capital: A Critique of Political Economy, vol. I* (1867), Chapter 26–31, Progress Publishers, Moscow, USSR; available at Marxist Internet Archive, https://www.marxists.org/archive/marx/works/1867-c1/.

Rosa Luxemburg, The Accumulation of Capital (1913), Chapter 27, The Accumulation of Capital; Edited by Dr. W. Stark, London, Routledge and Kegan Paul Ltd; 1951, available at Marxist Internet Archive, https://www.marxists.org/archive/luxemburg/1913/accumulation-capital/ch27.htm.

Angela Davis, "Reflections on the Black Woman's Role in the Community of Slaves," *The Black Scholar* (December 1971), 4–7, 12.

Robin D.G. Kelley, "Insecure: Policing Under Racial Capitalism," *Spectre Journal* (November 8, 2020), https://spectrejournal.com/insecure-policing-under-racial-capitalism/.

Letters from Vera Zasulich to Karl Marx (February 16 and March 8, 1881) / Marx-Zasulich Correspondence, In *Late Marx and the*

Russian Road, Marx and the 'peripheries of capitalism', edited by Teodor Shanin, Monthly Review Press, New York, 1983; available at Marxist Internet Archive, https://www.marxists.org/archive/marx/works/1881/zasulich/index.htm.

José Carlos Mariátegui, *Seven Interpretive Essays on Peruvian Reality* (Austin: University of Texas Press, 1971 [1927]); available at Marxist Internet Archive, https://www.marxists.org/archive/mariateg/works/7-interpretive-essays/index.htm.

Walter Rodney, *How Europe Underdeveloped Africa* (London: Verso, 2018), 9, 12, 36, 42–43, 53–54, 160–161.

W.E.B. Du Bois, *Black Reconstruction in America* (New York: Free Press, 1992). [Week 6] Ch. 1: 5, 12, 13, 15, 16; Ch. 2: 18, 20, 21, 26–27, 29–30; Ch. 4: 54–57, 67, 80, 82; Ch. 5: 109–110, 125–126. [Week 7]: Ch. 6: 131–132, 149; Ch. 7: 182–185, 188–189; Ch. 9: 325, 327, 345–346, 358, 367; Ch. 10: 381–383, 395–396, 399, 413, 428–429; Ch. 14: 623, 626, 630–631, 634–635; Ch. 16: 700–701, 703, 708.

Mumia Abu-Jamal, *We Want Freedom: A Life in the Black Panther Party* (Brooklyn, NY / Philadelphia, PA: Common Notions Press, 2016 [2004]).

Claude McKay, "If We Must Die" (July 1919), *The Liberator,* available at https://www.poetryfoundation.org/poems/44694/if-we-must-die

Refaat Alareer, "If I Must Die" (2023)

Frantz Fanon, *The Wretched of the Earth* (New York: Grove Press, [1961] 2004), 1–8.

EZLN, "First Declaration of the Lacandón Jungle" (1993), General Command of the EZLN, 31 December, available at Radio Zapatista, https://radiozapatista.org/?p=20280&lang=en.

Red Nation, *The Red Deal: Indigenous Action to Save Our Earth* (Brooklyn, NY / Philadelphia, PA: Common Notions Press, 2021).

V.I. Lenin, *The State and Revolution* (1917), Ch. 1, *Lenin: Collected Works, Volume 25*, p. 381–492 available at Marxist Internet Archive, https://www.marxists.org/archive/lenin/works/1917/staterev/

Joy James, *New Bones Abolition* (Brooklyn, NY / Philadelphia, PA: Common Notions Press, 2023), 15–17.

June Jordan, "Poem About Police Violence" [1978] In *Passion* (Beacon Press, 1980).

Geo Maher, *A World Without Police* (London: Verso, 2021), 23–28, 31–32.

Angela Davis, *Are Prisons Obsolete?* (New York: Seven Stories, 2003), 22–29, 32, 34–35, 37, 40–42, 44–45, 50, 55–56, 67–68, 84, 86–89, 91–93, 95, 100, 103–104.

Assata Shakur, "Women in Prison: How We Are," *Black Scholar* (April 1978), available at https://www.historyisaweapon.com/defcon1/shakurwip.html

Mariame Kaba, "Police 'Reforms' You Should Always Oppose," *TruthOut* (December 7th 2014), https://truthout.org/articles/police-reforms-you-should-always-oppose/.

Dean Spade, "No cops, courts, or cages means no state," *Contemporary Political Theory* 23, no. 1 (2024): 123–128.

Erica Caines, "Thoughts on Abolition," HoodCommunist.org (January 11, 2024), https://hoodcommunist.org/2024/01/11/thoughts-on-abolition/.

ABOUT THE W.E.B. DU BOIS MOVEMENT SCHOOL FOR ABOLITION & RECONSTRUCTION

The W.E.B. Du Bois Movement School for Abolition & Reconstruction is a political education program for aspiring revolutionaries and movement leaders from those communities most impacted by poverty, policing, and mass incarceration.

Our home is Philadelphia, crossroads of Harriet Tubman and Octavius Catto, W.E.B. Du Bois and Paul Robeson, Mumia Abu-Jamal and Maroon Shoatz, a critical hub for abolitionist militancy in the past and a thriving and powerful movement ecosystem today.

Through participatory and collective study of political economy, the history of global resistance movements, and the theoretical and practical aspects of social change, we aim to teach a new generation of organic intellectuals not only how to understand the world, but more importantly, how to *change* it.

https://abolitionschool.org

ABOUT COMMON NOTIONS

Common Notions is a publishing house and programming platform that fosters new formulations of living autonomy. We aim to circulate timely reflections, clear critiques, and inspiring strategies that amplify movements for social justice.

Our publications trace a constellation of critical and visionary meditations on the organization of freedom. By any media necessary, we seek to nourish the imagination and generalize common notions about the creation of other worlds beyond state and capital. Inspired by various traditions of autonomism and liberation—in the US and internationally, historical and emerging from contemporary movements—our publications provide resources for a collective reading of struggles past, present, and to come.

Common Notions regularly collaborates with political collectives, militant authors, radical presses, and maverick designers around the world. Our political and aesthetic pursuits are dreamed and realized with Antumbra Designs.

www.commonnotions.org
info@commonnotions.org

NOTES

NOTES